MURDER IN

Part Of The Proceeds From The Sale Of This Book Will Go To The Restoration Efforts Underway at the Sidna Allen House in Carroll County, Virginia. *(Photo Courtesy of Mark Harmon)*

LHP

Also by Thomas D. Perry

Ascent To Glory: The Genealogy of J. E. B. Stuart

The Free State of Patrick: Patrick County Virginia In The Civil War

"The Dear Old Hills of Patrick:" J. E. B. Stuart and Patrick County VA

Images of America: Patrick County Virginia

Images of America: Henry County Virginia

Then and Now: Patrick County Virginia

Notes From The Free State Of Patrick

God's Will Be Done: The Christian Life of J. E. B. Stuart

Patrick County Oral History Project: A Guide

Upward Toil: The Lester Family of Henry County Virginia

Mount Airy, North Carolina

Martinsville, Virginia

Henry County Heritage Book Volume One

Fieldale, Virginia

"If Thee Must Fight, Fight Well:" William J. Palmer

The Graham Mansion: A History

Beyond Mayberry: A Memoir of Andy Griffith and Mount Airy NC

A Dinky Railroad: The Mount Airy and Eastern Railway

Ghosts of the Graham Mansion

Visit www.freestateofpatrick.com for more information

Murder In A Rear View Mirror

Stories of True Crime

By

Thomas D. Perry

ISBN-13: 978-1523715589

ISBN-10: 1523715588

Laurel Hill Publishing

www.freestateofpatrick.com

Thomas D. "Tom" Perry
4443 Ararat Highway
P O Box 11
Ararat VA 24053

276-692-5300
freestateofpatrick@yahoo.com
www.freestateofpatrick.com

For Jennifer

Remember the victims of these stories as I remembered the victims at Virginia Tech on the tenth anniversary of their deaths on April 16, 2017.

"Our very freedom is secure because we're a nation governed by laws, not by men. We have the means to change the laws if they become unjust or onerous. We cannot, as citizens, pick and choose the laws we will or will not obey." RONALD REAGAN 9/3/1981

Jennifer Short

$67,000 REWARD OFFERED FOR INFORMATION LEADING TO ARREST AND CONVICTION

On August 15, 2002, at approximately 9:00 a.m., the bodies of Michael and Mary Short were discovered in their Bassett, Henry County, Virginia, home. Michael was found on the couch inside the attached garage of the home with an apparent gunshot wound to his head. His wife Mary was found lying in her bed and had suffered the same fate as her husband. The Short's 9-year-old daughter, Jennifer, was not located in the home and a search ensued for the missing child. Jennifer's remains were found on September 25, 2002, along a stream bed off Grogan Road, Stoneville, Rockingham County, North Carolina. It was determined that Jennifer's death was caused by a gunshot wound to the head. Law enforcement authorities continue to seek the public's help in locating the suspect(s) involved in the murders of Michael, Mary and their young daughter Jennifer Short.

IF YOU HAVE ANY INFORMATION CONCERNING THIS CASE, PLEASE CONTACT ANY OF THE FOLLOWING:
- **THE FBI BY LOGGING ONTO WWW.RICHMOND.FBI.GOV**
- **FBI TIP LINE AT 1-800-225-5324**
- **CRIMESTOPPERS AT 276-632-7463 OR 276-63CRIME**

Contents

Foreword: Murder In A Rear View Mirror   11

Chapter One: Fifty Hokies   19

Chapter Two: Martinsville's Fayette Street Shootout   47

Chapter Three: Stuart's Civil Rights Court Case   63

Chapter Four: Deadly Dentist   73

Chapter Five: The Martinsville Seven   95

Chapter Six: Ararat's Lynch Hollow   147

Chapter Seven: Lawson's Bloody Christmas   155

Chapter Eight: Mount Airy's Franklin Street Bomber   175

Chapter Nine: Revolutionary Murder In The Hollow   187

Chapter Ten: Tragedy At Fayerdale   209

Chapter Eleven: Murder In Kibler Valley   235

Chapter Twelve: Murder At Mount Airy Knitting   253

Chapter Thirteen: Where Is Gina Hall?   273

Chapter Fourteen: Two Sides: The Hillsville Shootout   289

Chapter Fifteen: Embracing Tragedy at Virginia Tech   347

Afterword: Curtains   379

Bibliography   385

Index   387

Scene of the murder in a rear view mirror in Collinsville, Virginia.

Foreword:

<u>MURDER IN A REAR VIEW MIRROR</u>

On a Saturday in May 1992, Jennifer Nickelston sat in a 1983 red Camaro on a gloriously sunny early summer day at a stop light in Collinsville, Virginia, just off Business 220 across from Najjar's Pizza in the parking lot of what is today the Dollar General Food Store. Earlier that day, she had been to the May Day program at her niece Adrienne's school program at Druid Hill's School.

Suddenly, from Jennifer's right came a car driven by an African-American male aged 34. I will not name the shooter and the victim out of respect for those family members who are still alive. Jennifer motioned him through, but he angrily did the same. She pulled up. There was one car in front of her at the light. At a quarter until four in the afternoon, Jennifer looked up in her rear-view mirror to a horrible sight.

The victim, an African-American female aged 27, the spouse of the man drove the car behind Jennifer. The wife saw her husband walking towards her after leaving his vehicle nearby. She quickly tried to back up, but struck the post at the Revco Drug Store, now Suit City. Her four-year-old daughter was in the car along with her twin sister, and her ten-year-old child.

From her rear-view mirror, Jennifer saw the man, walk up to the car behind her and shoot twice through the windshield with a 38-caliber revolver. He then walked to the side and shot once through the driver's side window. Jennifer saw blood hit the windshield inside the car behind her. Amazingly, the shooter did not injure the passengers.

Jennifer thought to herself, "I hope I am not next." At that moment two things occurred, the stoplight turned green, and Jennifer's survival instinct kicked in. She turned right on Business 220 and drove down to the nearby strip mall, where television channel BTW21 is today, turned around, and cautiously returned to see if she could help or talk to the police.

Off-duty Henry County Sheriff's Deputy, H. D. Linkous also saw the shooting but was unable to aid before the shooter got back in his car and shot himself in the shoulder for some unknown reason and drove off. Deputy Linkous communicated a description to authorities. Henry County Sheriff Cassell and another officer apprehended the shooter at the corner of Fayette and Alice Streets. They carried the shooter to the hospital for treatment and then took him to jail.

The shooter had one earlier conviction for assault. The shooter and his estranged wife, the victim, both worked at Sara Lee Knit Products, where she worked in the sewing room, and he worked in the warehouse. She refused to reconcile and moved from their home on Alice Street.

The family tried to get the victim to change her personalized license plates that allowed the shooter to stalk her easily. The family commented on the situation in *the Martinsville Bulletin* that he had a "nasty attitude" about her and that they "kept telling her he was going to do it." Another commented that "We didn't think he was crazy enough to do it. I guess we were wrong." The family said that the victim had been to the "police" many times warning them the shooter had a gun, which I expect was not legal for a convicted felon. Gun laws not enforced do no good for the victims of gun violence and such was the result in this case. She died at 4:15 p.m.

Murder in a rear view mirror is a metaphor for looking back on the stories of true crime contained in this book. Jennifer Nickelston Gregory gave me the idea for this book by telling me her story and encouraged me with others, even researching some of them.

When men ignore God's law and man's law to take the law into their own hands, there are consequences. Taking another human being's life is a mortal sin in the eyes of man and God, but in the heat of the moment when a man's blood is up, reactions take the place of wisdom. As Proverbs states, "Pride goes before destruction, And a haughty spirit before stumbling." Simply said, "Pride cometh before a fall." When you add alcohol, guns, and years of built-up frustration nothing good happens, but more often mental health issues have come to the forefront when it comes to this violence.

This book is about murder in a rear-view mirror as I look back on stories of true crime that have interested me over the years. These stories take place along the North Carolina and Virginia state lines near the place I was born, Mount Airy, North Carolina, and the place I spent my formative years, Ararat, Patrick County, Virginia.

These essays, based on true stories as the movies say, are about real people, who made choices in the heat of the moment and sometimes planned. These are stories of sick minds and angry men who reacted before they thought, but we all should remember what the "Good Book" says that you should not murder because the law speaks of justified killing when the perpetrators violate the law, man's, and God's. There are consequences for those who take another life. "You shall not murder."

I based many of these essays on the questions people ask me about at the myriads of events I attend during the years selling books. One chapter is about a courthouse shootout. Growing up near Hillsville, Virginia, one could not escape the "Shootout" at the Carroll County Courthouse from 1912. Recently, it was the subject of a play by Frank Levering and a symposium in

2012 in the same room where the killing occurred in 1912. It was while attending these events I seriously thought about this book, so it is right that the cover reflects that with the Sidna Allen House and the one essay tells that story. These essays revolve around the theme of what drives people to take the law into their own hands and to take the life of another human being. No one in a civilized society has that right.

The saying among journalists is that "murder sells" and so it is among publishers too. Some of the proceeds from this book will go to the restoration efforts underway at the Sidna Allen house in Carroll County, Virginia. While murder sells, it can also preserve the history of our region.

Efforts are underway to preserve the Sidna Allen House

Hokie Bird mourns on the tenth anniversary of the Virginia Tech shootings on April 16, 2017.

Chapter One:

<u>FIFTY HOKIES</u>

When you write of true crime, it is important to share events that interest you personally or are close to your own life. No event made a bigger impression on me than the shootings at my alma mater, Virginia Tech. This event is still fresh in my mind and the lives of those involved. In researching this first chapter, I discovered that I knew very little about what happened in Blacksburg, Virginia. While being keenly aware that the survivors of the shootings are still alive as are the families of the victims, who lost their lives that day, I feel that telling this story is important and how things have changed and not changed since the tragic events of a decade ago.

Seung Hui Cho was born in 1984 in South Korea. He underwent treatment at age three for heart problems, which seemed to traumatize him making him shy, frail, and wary of physical contact. When he was eight, he came with his family to the United States in 1992. His family settled in Centreville, Virginia, in Fairfax County, where his family ran a dry-cleaning business.

By 1997, Cho showed signs of mental illness as he was quiet and did not like to interact with people and at times refused to speak. Teachers became concerned as he was introverted and friendless. Diagnosed with severe depression and selective mutism, he received counseling in middle school and received a diagnosis of a social anxiety disorder that inhibited his speech. He took therapy and took antidepressants throughout middle school.

In 1999, Columbine High School in Colorado was the scene of a shooting that left twelve students dead, one teacher killed, and 21 students wounded. Cho became obsessed with this mass shooting. The following year Cho received a diagnosis of "emotional disability," but he improved to the point that doctors took him off his medication by July 2000.

Bullied in high school due to his speech difficulties, teachers excused Cho from discussions. He underwent art therapy and medication. He graduated with a 3.5 GPA in 2003. His family and school counselors urged him to stay close to home in a small college environment so that they could address his needs, but he insisted on going to Virginia Tech, where he was far away from home with no support system like he had in high school. Due to privacy laws, no one informed Virginia Tech of his mental health issues, and no one at Virginia Tech asked. Cho was 18 and an adult under the law.

Described as very neat, his parents called him every Sunday. He ignored his roommates or responded with single word responses. Cho moved off campus as a sophomore, developed an interest in writing as his grades began to slip. He started as a computer major as a freshman but switched to English as a junior in 2005. Many close to him thought was a strange choice considering his inability to communicate and that the classes would be small with lots of expectations of self-expression and participation.

Cho was not athletic and did not take part in extracurricular activities. He lived very "frugally" and never asked for extra money from his parents. His parents often visited in his freshman year, but these visits became less as time went on. His parents could not read English well and did not read his controversial writings that became darker and more violent during his time at Virginia Tech.

In Spring 2005, a publisher rejected a novel he wrote. He became "withdrawn and hostile." As spring turned to fall in 2005, Cho moved back on campus, but his interactions became more troubling. At a party, he stabbed a carpet repeatedly with a knife. Over the years, his suitemates noted he watched movies on his laptop, played basketball alone, but did not play video games. He wrote heavy metal lyrics on walls and along hallways and even made up a twin brother.

He wore a baseball cap and dark reflector "aviator" type sunglasses to class. Teachers asked Cho to remove them. He received reprimands for harassing multiple female students. He was very quiet and gave very short answers in class. He read violent poems in class and was taking pictures of female classmates without their permission. Many of his classmates were afraid of Cho. In October, Professor Nikki Giovanni wrote a letter to Cho about his behavior in her class.

Giovanni informed the English Department Head Lucinda Roy that she wanted Cho removed from her class. Roy contacted Virginia Tech Police Detective George Jackson about Cho and urged him to get counseling, which required him to come to the counseling center. Roy also contacted multiple parties including the Associate Dean of the Liberal Arts and Human Science, the Vice-President and Dean of Student Affairs, and the Cook Counseling Center. Roy received permission to remove Cho from Giovanni's class if there was a "viable alternative." Roy began to tutor Cho one on one. Cho refused counseling.

In November, Cho's roommates thought he set fires in the lounge of their dorm. A female West Ambler Johnston resident filed reports about Cho contacting her online, via phone, and in person, but declined to press charges. At the end of the month the Cook Counseling Center "triaged" Cho over the phone, but not in person.

The following month more complaints from female students continued including Instant Messages using foul language. He even wrote messages on the message boards on doors of female student's rooms. One of them came from Shakespeare's Romeo and Juliet. "By a name, I know not how to tell thee who I am, my name, dear saint is hateful to myself, because it is an enemy to thee, Had I it written, I would tear the word." After complaints, Cho claimed that "Shakespeare did it."

He missed appointments with counselors and or was again, "triaged" over the phone. His behavior was escalating towards a crisis, which occurred on December 13, 2005. Cho threatened suicide saying, "I might as well kill myself now." Police took Cho into custody overnight after a judge ordered mandatory outpatient treatment and committed him to Carilion St. Albans Psychiatric Hospital, but no one contacted his family. A staffer at the New River Valley Community Services Board (NRVCSB) thought he was "an imminent danger to his self and others." A psychiatrist and a psychologist believed Cho from his conversations and found him not to be a danger and ordered outpatient treatment for him, which he attended once. No one

from the NRVCSB came to his commitment hearing on December

14. He was an adult, and privacy laws prevented this sort of action

by the school or mental health officials as they feared lawsuits. No

one notified Cho's parents. There was no follow up from staff and

no system centralized. No one collected "collateral information"

about his other mental problems. Cho made an appointment for

counseling and was released. His parents expressed later, they

would have pulled him out of Virginia Tech, if they had known

about his sinking into oblivion.

In January, the Cook Counseling Center received a

summary from St. Albans about Cho, but no one followed up. Dr.

Miller of CCC left his position and took Cho's file home with him

by mistake, where it remained until July 2009, after the

settlement with the families of the Virginia Tech shootings.

As 2006 turned into spring, Cho became more isolated,

and his grades fluctuated. He dropped classes and had

altercations with professors, who did not report the incident. One

professor said that Cho knew how to "play the game, do as little as he needed to do to get by." His drawings and writings turned bleak under the obsession he had with the school killings. His writings continued to show violence, and, in the fall, he wrote a play about a school shooting that struck very close to his future actions. Professors reported Cho to an Associate Dean, who found no mention of earlier mental health issues. She encouraged Cho to seek counseling, which he declined.

Under Federal law, he was ineligible to buy guns due to mental health issues, but the authorities did not list Cho in the system. Gun laws only work if officials enforce them. Cho slipped through the cracks of the system.

In February 2007, he bought his first gun, a .22 caliber Walther P22 online and picked it up at a local pawn shop. Virginia had a law of one gun per month. He bought a Glock 19, a 9-mm handgun, at a Roanoke gun shop in March. At the same time, he rented a van for a month that he used to videotape his "diatribes." He used a credit card for these purchases, and his parents did not get the bills until after his death.

Federal law disqualified Cho from gun purchases because of his "adjudicated as a mental defect or who has been committed to a mental institution." As noted, he spent a night at St. Albans. Virginia law is more "murky" about the legality of his gun purchases.

He began to buy ammunition in small amounts online at eBay, Wal-Mart, and Dick's Sporting Goods. He choose 9mm hollow point rounds of ammunition to increase the severity of the wounds. eBay later stopped the purchase of ammo online. There were no restrictions on ammo purchases.

Cho violated laws and the policy at Virginia Tech, but if no one connects the dots or enforces the law, laws, and policies do no good when dealing with a person with obvious mental instability and the ambition to wreak such havoc on a college campus.

On April 8, 2017, he checked into a Hampton Inn to do more videotaping as he continued to buy ammunition systematically. Five days later Virginia Tech received bomb threats to three separate buildings, Torgersen, Durham, and Whittemore

Halls. There were no lockdowns or evacuations. Some thought Cho called them in to see what the reaction would be to the threats. The next day witnesses saw him practicing chaining the doors to Norris Hall. On April 15, he called his parents for their weekly Sunday night conversation. They noted nothing unusual in his behavior.

On Monday, April 16, 2007, Virginia Tech had 26,000 students out of a total of 34,000 persons on campus. There were 131 buildings on 2,600 acres. Sixteen different roads allowed access to campus that had 35 police officers. It had an email system in place with 96% of the campus connected with 36,000 email addresses. It took about twenty minutes for the local media to broadcast a message. There was an Emergency Response Plan, but no shooting scenario and the police did not have the power to lock down the campus. It had to come from the administration of the university.

At 6:47 a.m., witnesses saw Cho loitering at the entrance to West Ambler Johnston Hall (WAJ). His mailbox was in the foray of the building, but he could not enter the building until 10 a.m. or the main residence hall at all with his key card.

Virginia Tech named the dorm that is home to over 800 students for James Markham Ambler Johnston in 1969. Johnston, an architectural engineer, a Civil War authority, and was responsible for the original preservation of many of the battlefields around Richmond, Virginia, where the Hokie alum resided and for bringing Civil War Historian James I. Robertson, Jr. to Virginia Tech.

Freshman Emily Hilscher, age 19, entered her dorm at 7:02 a.m. Her boyfriend, Karl Thornhill, a Radford student, dropped her off as he often did on Monday mornings. Emily made her way to her Room 4040. There has never been any connection between Hilscher and Cho at this writing. It was "sad coincidence" that she was the person that Cho met that morning.

The first victim shows this writer what a small world it can be. Emily was a high school student of a friend of mine, Melissa Weeks, at Rappahannock High School. Known as "Pixie," Emily was a member of the equestrian team at Virginia Tech.

Between 7:05 and 7:12, Cho shot Hilscher and Ryan Clark. Emily survived for three hours, but no one notified her family in Rappahannock County until after her death. They found out when Emily's boyfriend Karl Thornhill's mother contacted them. A Fed Ex driver also told the parents too, but no one from Virginia Tech contacted them. When her father contacted the local hospital, officials told him a "Jane Doe" came from Virginia Tech to a Roanoke hospital.

Senior Ryan Christopher Clark, age 22, was the Resident Advisor on the fourth floor and lived in Room 4042. He was working on a triple major at Virginia Tech of English, Biology, and Psychology. He was an active member of the Marching Virginians. It is this author's opinion that Clark was the first of many Hokie heroes that day when he went to Emily Hilscher's defense.

Virginia Tech police received a phone call from the West Ambler Johnson Residence Hall (WAJ) on the campus at 7:20 a.m. The caller told Police a student might have fallen out of their bed in Room 4040, but first responders arrived to discover two wounded students and a blood trail leaving the dorm room, which indicated the shooter was at large on the campus. First responders are there at 7:21-7:24 a.m. including rescue squad and police. Throughout this horrible day in the history of Virginia Tech, the first responders were top notch in their response to the shootings.

At 8:00 a.m. classes began as Virginia Tech Police Chief Wendell Flinchum arrived at WAJ along with members of the Blacksburg, Virginia Tech, and Virginia State Police. At 8:11 a.m., Flinchum talked to Virginia Tech President Charles Steger to inform him of the situation including the fact that someone shot two students and one was dead. Police found thirteen bloody footprints, size ten, leaving the building along with a bloody thumbprint on the stairwell door handle leaving to the outside of the building. Steger's secretary knew about it at 8:10 a.m. He asked her to get Chief Flinchum on the phone. President Steger knew at 8:11 a.m. the situation at WAJ, and for one hour nothing happened.

Steger convened Virginia Tech's Policy Group in his Burruss Hall office at 8:25 a.m. Word was across the campus. The Virginia

Tech Center for Professional and Continuing Education locked down on its own at 8:00 a.m. Thirty minutes earlier a housekeeper in WAJ notified a fellow housekeeper in Burruss Hall. A member of the Policy Group informed a colleague in Richmond that one student was dead, one critically wounded, and the "Gunman is on the loose."

At 8:14 a.m. Heather Hough, the roommate of Emily Hilscher, arrived at room 4040. For the next thirty minutes, police interviewed her. From Hough, they found out that Emily's boyfriend dropped her off on Monday mornings and then went to class at nearby Radford University. Police learned that he owned a gun and by 8:30, Thornhill is a "person of interest." Flinchum informs Steger of this, but the latter later that day claimed to know an hour earlier. No one asked Hough about a potential "love triangle" or the potential that the "incident" was of a domestic nature. Published sources reported that Clark was gay and was not interested in Hilscher.

At 8:50, the Policy Group claimed they were unable to send a message across campus due to a technical problem. Two

32

minutes later, Blacksburg Public Schools locked down. Eight

minutes later the Virginia Tech Veterinarian College locked down

on its own. Virginia Tech stopped trash pickup and bank deposits,

but classes continued across campus.

Flinchum claimed later that he did not have the power to

order a lockdown of the campus and did not raise the issue to

Steger. Later many thought the lack of a reaction was due to the

incident that happened on August 20, 2006. On that day police

transported William Morva, an inmate, from the Blacksburg jail to

Montgomery Regional Hospital for treatment of a sprained ankle

and wrist. After using a bathroom, Morva knocked out a deputy

and killed a hospital security guard. Virginia Tech canceled classes

and locked down the campus even though the suspect was never

on campus. Police captured Morva. Steger claimed in April 2007,

he did not want to cause a similar panic, but there is no evidence

that such a panic occurred in 2006.

At 9:05 a.m., police allowed two students in WAJ, Henry

Lee, and Rachel Hill, to leave the dorm for their classes, which were in Norris Hall Room 206, a French class that neither would survive that day.

Radford Police pulled over Karl Thornhill, Emily Hilscher's boyfriend at 9:24 a.m. Six minutes later, Thornhill underwent a gunshot residue test that was negative. Later that day, police served a search warrant at his apartment, where they handcuffed and forced Thornhill, not too gently, to the floor. In Harper Hall, Cho's roommates received similar treatment.

At 9:26 a.m. Virginia Tech sent out an email alert informing students, staff, and faculty of an incident at WAJ and reported that it was an isolated incident and domestic in nature. There was no evidence of a domestic incident and the emphasis on Thornhill because he owned a gun led to an incredible loss of life. The message reported no one killed or wounded or no hint of a shooter still at large. At 9:30, police informed the Policy Group that Thornhill is not the "likely" shooter.

Seung Hui Cho, age 23, returned to his room in Harper Hall at 7:17 a.m. and changed clothes. He deleted his email accounts and computer files. Investigators never found his hard drive and cell phone but suspected he threw it in the Duck Pond on the west end of campus.

At 9:01 a.m. Cho mailed a package to NBC in New York City at the downtown Blacksburg Post Office. The package held an 1,800 word "rant." There were DVDs with twenty-seven videos holding scenes and images of Cho posing with his guns reading his statement. He called the Columbine shooters "martyrs" and likened himself to Jesus. He hated wealthy kids and their "debauchery" saying they were deceitful charlatans. He said, "You had a hundred billion chances and ways to have avoided today."

Across campus at Norris Hall, an accounting class on the third floor were taking an exam. On the second floor, classes were taking place in five rooms including engineering, French, and German. Virginia Tech named the building "in 1967 for Earle Bertram Norris, dean of engineering and director of the Engineering Experiment Station from 1928 to 1952. Called indispensable by Virginia Tech's president, Norris chaired the Administrative Council, started off-campus engineering programs that evolved into new colleges, doubled the curricula in

35

engineering, helped organize a Student Engineering Council, and co-wrote three textbooks. His service as a lieutenant colonel in World War I drew praise from General John J. Pershing."

Cho walked across campus with his backpack full of chains, locks, a hammer, knife, two guns, and 19 magazines holding 400 rounds of ammunition. Between 9:15 and 9:30, witnesses saw Cho outside Norris Hall. Upon entering the building, Cho chained shut the three main doors to the building and left a note warning of a bomb if anyone opened the doors. Cho had a class in Norris Hall, but not a Monday class.

Room 206 was graduate engineering class in Advance Hydrology Engineering that lost the Professor G. V. Logathan and nine students while injuring three more. Two students survived unhurt. Logathan shielded student Guillermo Colman from a severe injury while losing his own life. Another wounded student, Waleed Shaalan, tried to distract Cho but was shot and lost his life.

Loganathan born at the southern tip of India in 1954 and came to Virginia Tech in 1981 after receiving his Ph.D. from

Purdue University in water supply distribution in municipalities. Another Hokie hero lost his life.

Room 207 was a German class that lost a Professor Jamie Bishop with ten of twelve students shot, four of them died, and six were wounded. Student Derek O'Dell described Cho quiet with a blank expression and as "very calm, very determined, methodical." O'Dell did not realize he was wounded until after he blocked the door to the classroom with classmate Katelyn Carney.

Christopher James "Jamie" Bishop born in Pine Mountain, Georgia, in 1971, received his BA and MA degrees from the University of Georgia. He spent four years in Germany, where he met and married Stephanie Hofer. He taught at UNC-Chapel Hill until 2004, when he came to Virginia Tech. He wanted to change the world with art. He was a multi-media artist, graphic designer, and photographer.

Cho shot students Michael Pohle and Nicole White in the front row and then made his way down a row methodically shooting and wounded six more students. The dead bodies of Pohle and White were found embracing.

Room 205 was a class on Issues in Scientific Computing. Haiyon Cheng was substituting for the professor that day. Cho tried to push in the door, but students blocked it with a desk. He shot through the door and moved on to another classroom. Cho never got into Room 205.

Room 211 was a French class that lost the Professor Jocelyne Couture-Novak and eleven students with six more wounded. Those in Room 211 heard shots and mistook them for construction. Student Henry Lee saw the notice of a shooter on campus on his computer. He lived in West Ambler Johnston, and police allowed him to go to class that morning. Professor Novak looked out in the hall, turned around, and told everyone to get under their desks. The professor placed a desk in front of the door, but Cho pushed in and began shooting as he walked up and down the rows of students.

Another Hokie hero from that day was Matthew La Porte, a member of the Virginia Tech Corps of Cadets, who received eight bullets as he moved forward to try and stop Cho. He received full military honors at burial.

Cho shot a student in the leg after a call to 911. Another student hid a phone in her hair. Cho shot her twice in the head, but she miraculously survived. She kept the phone on and "played possum" along with other students who survived. Survivors told how they saw Cho dressed in boots, khaki pants, white shirt, and a holster.

At 9:41 a.m., Blacksburg Police got a call and transferred it to Virginia Tech Police. Four minutes later police arrived at Norris Hall and found the doors chained shut and heard shots. Next door in Burruss Hall, President Steger heard the shots from his office.

Cho returned to Room 207 and could not get inside. He returned to Room 211 and again walked up and down the rows shooting. One student was not injured but pretended to be dead to save his life. A janitor saw Cho reloading one of his guns and went back downstairs to the first floor.

Room 204 was an engineering class on mechanics led by Professor Liviu Librescu, a Holocaust survivor, who blocked the door with his body and yelled at his students to go out the windows. Ten students escaped through a window after pushing out screens and jumping 19 feet below to the bushes and grass. Senior Caroline Merrey said, "I don't think I would be here if it wasn't for Librescu." Cho killed the professor by shooting him five times. He shot killed another student, Minal Panchal, and wounded three other students.

Librescu, born in Romania in 1930 before finding himself in a "Jewish Ghetto," while his father went to a labor camp during World War II. He studied Aeronautical Engineering at the University of Bucharest. He was a researcher at the Bucharest Institute of Applied Mechanics for nearly twenty years. He moved to Israel in 1978 after he refused to swear allegiance to the Communist Party in Romania, and spent over three years trying to get permission to immigrate. He taught at Tel Aviv University before coming to Virginia Tech in 1985 for a one-year sabbatical and never went back to Israel to teach. Age 76, he was a Professor of Engineering Science and Mechanics. He rests today in Israel. On April 18, 2007, President George W. Bush honored Librescu at the Holocaust Memorial Museum in Washington D. C.

Professor Kevin Granata came down from the third floor and lost his life after he took twenty students to his office and locked it. None of them were hurt. Another Professor, Wally Grant, was shot by Cho but survived.

Granata, born in 1961, was a leading faculty in biomechanics, who had cerebral palsy. He received his BA and Ph.D. from Ohio State University and his MA at Purdue University, where he met his wife, Linda Ankenman. They had three children together. At Virginia Tech, he taught in the Department of Engineering Science and Mechanics. He also had connections to the Wake Forest University School of Biomedical Engineering and the University of Virginia's Department of Orthopedic Surgery.

At 9:50 a.m., police used shotguns to open an entrance to the machine shop in Norris Hall, which was not chained by the shooter. They heard gunshots and proceeded up to the second floor. At that same time, an email was sent to the Virginia Tech community informing the students, staff, and faculty that "A gunman is loose on campus. Advising everyone to stay in buildings until further notice and avoid the windows." Four outside speakers broadcasted the message.

At 9:51 a.m. Cho returned to the Room 211 for the third time. There he took his own life as police reached the second floor. The room held eleven dead, four wounded, and one student unhurt. At 10:08 a.m. police discovered Cho's dead body in Room 211 with two weapons and no identification.

In eleven minutes, he shot 174 rounds, killing thirty people, wounding seventeen before killing himself. He still had 203 rounds left, 122 for the Glock and 81 for the Walther. Police found seventeen empty ammo magazines. Each held 10 to 15 shots.

Five faculty and twenty-seven students lost their lives. Six were injured jumping from Norris Hall. Cho shot seventeen, but they survived. There were 46 people on the third floor of Norris Hall unhurt.

In the fall of 2006, Cho wrote a play about "a young man who hates the students at his school and plans to kill them and himself." He described his plan in a playwriting class, but this was not make believe, this was a tragedy that never should have happened.

First responders to Norris Hall came face to face with the loss or wounding that day of fifty Hokies and the heartbreaking realization of texts and phone calls that remained unanswered as phones vibrated in the Norris and West Ambler Johnston Halls.

Campus maps showing the locations of the buildings involved in the Virginia Tech shootings on April 16, 2007.

Top of the Virginia Tech Chapel.

Advertisement for Spencer Brother's Tobacco.

Chapter Two:

MARTINSVILLE'S FAYETTE STREET SHOOTOUT

Gunfire erupted on May 17, 1886, in Martinsville, Virginia, in one of the largest gunfights ever recorded on the east coast. The shootout ended with nine people shot and three dead including an African-American bystander. It was just five years after Wyatt Earp and the Gunfight at the OK Corral, but that was thousands of miles away in the western frontier town of Tombstone, Arizona. The shooting in Martinsville happened within sight of the Henry County Court House in the middle of a quiet southern town on Fayette Street.

Aiken Summit along the Danville and Western Railroad was home to the Terrys. Their home, Marr's Hill, and Terry's Mountain were marks they left on the landscape of Henry County, Virginia, but in the late 1880s, tradition says their prospects were on the way down. The children of Parker and Mary King Terry lived on land granted them from colonial times.

The Spencers were a family on the rise in the summer of 1886. Their home was Grassdale on the western side of Henry County. These two families met as their lines of ascent and descent crossed on the streets of Martinsville.

D. H. Spencer and Sons moved their tobacco operation to Fayette Street within sight of the Henry County Court House. Their brands included Calhoun and Old Crow. The company was one of the first to make their own boxes for shipment. Peter Spencer was on the Martinsville Town Council. On May 8, 1886, the council heard complaints from two fertilizers agents, A. W. Hill and B. F. Barrow, who thought their annual license tax discriminated against their product. They did not get the two-thirds vote needed to change their bill with Mayor C. B. Bryant and "Colonel Peter" Spencer voting against them.

The Editor of the *Henry News*, J. T. Darlington, published an anonymous article that was an obvious satire of the meeting. The article written by local attorney William King Terry, who may have represented the fertilizer agents, made fun of Bryant and Spencer. On Saturday, May 15, Terry distributed a printed circular that was more critical of the two men. One author speculates that it looks like an "overreaction" or an "emotional" response by Terry that may show some existing bad blood between the Spencers and Terrys already existed.

The following day, the story goes, May 16, a Sunday, Peter Spencer printed up a poster comparing Terry to a jackass. John Hardin Pedigo, who wrote for both sides, "ghost wrote" the poster. Attempts to destroy the posters were not completely successful as William Terry found one. "Finding himself effectively called an SOB, Will Terry was enraged." It was a time of honor and reputation in the two decades since the end of the Civil War, and with the recent death of his father, Terry could not ignore the slander. He lived in a local hotel in Martinsville and the small world the town would have been at that time made conflict and stirring the pot of controversy a good sport for some in those days as cable television sensationalizes today's rumors and innuendo.

Terry distributed another circular. The printer, Darlington at the *Henry News*, certainly was busy. It read, "I have been attacked by some low contemptable scoundrel and midnight

49

assassin, by the publication of an anonymous card. If, however, he will present himself he shall receive the chastisement he so richly merits."

On Monday, May 17, Terry learned that the *Henry News* printed Peter Spencer's circular. He sent word to his brothers, Jake and Ben Terry, who soon arrived on a railroad in Martinsville. Noting the heightened tension, more "peace officers" than usual were present including the Sheriff, several deputies, two constables, and a town sergeant.

At 7 p.m., employees streamed out of the Spencer Tobacco plant on Fayette Street, where they worked from sunrise to sunset. When Peter and John Spencer came out, William Terry called and asked Peter directly if he wrote the "horse card." Peter answered that he did. Terry grabbed his pistol, but W. H. Werth grabbed Terry. John Spencer suggested that there were "other means for handling the dispute." J. T. Darlington pointed out that the Spencers outnumbered the Terrys, as the Spencers had five gunmen present due to "prior arrangements." Seeing the situation William Terry stepped away with Darlington.

As with all such situations, it only takes one person to create a catastrophe, and many believe that person was Tarleton Brown. Smoke filled the air for about twenty-five feet around the entrance to the Spencer Tobacco Company. The Richmond Dispatch noted, "at least a dozen revolvers flashed in the air. The death dealing missiles flew thick and fast, rarely missing their prey. Every man stood his ground with nerve and grit." Gilmore Dickinson shot Will Terry in the back "fifteen inches away." Ben Terry shot Tarleton Brown after the latter fired at Jake Terry.

The shootout wounded nine people. All three Terry brothers were down. Jake died at once. Will died after lingering several weeks and Ben, hit twice, once in the neck, recovered. Peter Spencer, shot in the ribs, survived for five years. Bystanders J. R. Gregory and an African-American Sandy Martin lost their lives.

Shot were "Peace Officers" Hugh N. Dyer and B. L. Jones. Hugh Nelson Dyer went on to become Roanoke Chief of Police and wrote a memoir of the event. Born on November 28, 1860, in Henry County, the son of W. C. Dyer, Hugh served as a Police Chief and Sergeant for five years in Martinsville. He went to Roanoke in 1889 and on December 20, 1893, became the Chief of Police. That same year, he married Emma Hutchinson. He died on August 5, 1936, in Staunton and rests today in Roanoke's Fairview Cemetery.

The *Halifax Advertiser* reported three days after the gunfight that, "Jake Terry was shot in the side and killed. Colonel P. D. Spencer was wounded in the right side, T. F. Brown shot painfully in the thigh, W. K. Terry shot in the left shoulder near the spinal column, Ben Terry shot in the bowels and neck, B. L. Jones painfully wounded in the thigh, Hugh Dyer shot in the thigh, two men by the name of Gregory were shot in the back accidentally, and a colored man by the name of Martin was shot in the thigh."

The *Henry News* of June 24 reported testimony of Darlington this way. "J. T. Darlington: - There was a difficulty on Fayette Street on May 17, 1886. After the difficulty had progressed a very few seconds, shots being fired by other parties, I saw G. G. Dickinson, who was then standing about three feet in the rear of W. K. Terry. While in that position a pistol in

Dickinson's hand was fired, and W. K. Terry fell. This is about all I know."

Cross-examined by G. L. Richardson for Commonwealth: "I afterward saw W. K. Terry; did not then examine his wound, but have done so since. I think the muzzle of the pistol was not more than fifteen feet... (I am not sure whether the following is referring to W. K. Terry, but it seems appropriate) lower limbs are paralyzed. I think his condition critical. He has completely lost the use of his legs. The last time I saw him I could see no real improvement, but a perceptible loss of strength."

The court fined Ben Terry $20 and costs for carrying a concealed weapon. A judge dismissed all other charges. The Terry daughters moved on top of Terry Mountain due to the shame of the shootout. None of the ten Terry children ever married.

It was the time of the Hatfields and McCoys in neighboring West Virginia, who had been feuding for three years when the gunfire erupted in Henry County. It was over a decade before the Allens shot up the Carroll County Court House in Hillsville. The story of the gunfight even reached the *New York*

Times, which at least three separate stories about it including the gunfight, subsequent trial and on August 31, 1886, reporting the death of W. K. Terry, who lingered from May until his death the day before the article.

Lost in the story is the murder of a "young farmer," R. H. Bowsman of "Horse Pasture," in September that resulted in an indictment of J. V. Darlington, who was still instigating in the matter and a trial in November with the jury finding the latter not guilty. The newspaper reported that Darlington's son and Bowsman were "in difficulty."

Another story reported on September 11 that a "large number of citizens of the county met and organized for the purpose of lynching Spencer, Brown, Dickerson, and Darlington...The plan failed through one of the members of the band, who betrayed the whole thing. People of the town and county are worked up over the affair. Nearly every man in Martinsville has been sworn as a special officer. It is whispered around that the failure of the lynching plan is for a short time; the enraged citizens will eventually carry out their intentions."

This story did not die even though many locals wish it would. Years later a magazine writer, Hiram Herbert, wrote a story for *Saga Magazine: Adventure Stories For Men*. When no locals would talk with him other than Gus Dyer, the son of Hugh, Herbert resorted to sensationalizing the story by interjecting a romance between May Belle Spencer or Belle Spencer and Will Terry. There was no romance nor was there a Belle Spencer.

Born on September 16, 1861, Tarleton F. Brown died on May 8, 1895, nearly a decade after the shootout on Fayette Street. After his death in 1895, and his wife Annie Eliza Brown (1862-1901) six years later, Henry Clay Lester and his wife Lucy "Big Lucy" Brown Lester, sister of Tarleton, raised her brother's children Rives S. Brown, Lucy Brown "Little Lucy," and Mattie T. Brown. The latter married George M. Andes and was the father of the recently deceased Tarleton River Andes. When "Big Lucy" died she left the Lanier Farm to Rives Brown, Sr., and his sister, "Little Lucy."

Rives Spotswood Brown, Sr. (1894-1957), a graduate of Randolph-Macon, became a prominent man of Martinsville. When

Henry Clay Lester died in 1913, Brown took over management of Lester's business interest. On May 20, 1916, Brown married Cornelia Frances Gregory, and they had a son Rives S. Brown, Jr. on August 30, 1919.

Lucy Gaines Brown "Little Lucy" (1888-1926) married Dr. Morton Elbridge Hundley. After Lucy's death, Dr. Hundley married Mary Kate Black (1896-1944) in November 1927 at the age of 49. Hundley died on his honeymoon of pneumonia in Switzerland, but that is another story.

Rives S. Brown, Sr. began his first development on Mulberry Road in 1925. In 1930, Rives S. Brown, Sr. built the Chief Tassell Building and five years later the Rives Theatre, Kroger's Grocery, and the Greyhound Bus Station. Three years later in 1938, he came up with a plan for Forest Park.

Among other holdings inherited from Henry Clay Lester, "the wealthiest man in Henry County at the time," was the Lanier Farm that Brown farmed until 1922. The Marshall Hairston Lanier Farm had a storied history, which was once the property of Patrick Henry, who sold the property to David Lanier, until today where the 2,000 acres is the site of the Druid Hills and Forest Park residential areas.

The legacy of the "Shootout on Fayette Street" continues with the Spencers, Terrys, Lesters, and Browns as they continue to make a mark on the landscape of Martinsville and Henry County Virginia. As with all things related to Henry County and Martinsville's history you need to travel to the Bassett Historical Center, where you will find files and even a privately published book about the "Shootout on Fayette Street."

The old Henry County Courthouse at the intersection of Fayette
Street in Martinsville was within sight of the shootings.

The Virginia Historical Highway Marker denotes the African-American history along Fayette Street including the Baldwin Block denoted on the next page.

Fayette Street looking towards the old Henry County Courthouse.

Kittie Reynolds was the mother of the sons involved in the next murder case that went all the way to the Supreme Court.

Chapter Three:

STUART'S CIVIL RIGHTS COURT CASE

Two articles from The *New York Times* on April 12, 1879, and October 16, 1879, discuss the most famous court case held in the Patrick County Courthouse. The Patrick County Courthouse joined the Virginia Landmarks Register on September 17, 1974, and the National Register of Historic Places on December 27, 1974. Patrick County came into existence on June 1, 1791. Twelve days later, the first court met at the home of Jonathan Hanby. Partitioned from Henry County in 1790, Patrick County included 458 square miles. Later land went to Franklin, Grayson, and Carroll counties.

In 1792, Eliphaz Shelton donated ten acres including the land where the Patrick County Courthouse now sits. In April 1793, the "Gentlemen Justices" of Patrick County authorized the construction of the building. The structure was to be thirty-six feet long and twenty-four feet wide with two twelve-foot jury rooms heated by fireplaces with plastered walls and eighteen "lights" of glass in the windows. Contractor Charles Vest completed his work before the deadline, and the courthouse opened for the court in October 1794. For the next twenty-five years, the building served the county.

In 1819, the county authorized a new building, but two years passed before construction began. Abram Staples, one of the justices, built the new courthouse had the new structure ready one year and one month later on July 11, 1822. Four major renovations have occurred since 1822. In 1928, saw the Sheriff's Office and jail added. Remodeling occurred in 1936 and 1972. In 1982, another renovation began to relocate the General District Court, Juvenile and Domestic Relations Court, the Circuit Court Judge's secretary and to add space for the Patrick County Clerk of Court's office.

The building is of Roman Revival or Jeffersonian Neo-Classic in style and made of red brick with a "central three bay blocks and two flanking wings." There are four Tuscan columns and a large stairway leading from the ground to the portico. This reflects the "high basements" of the Roman Revival. There is a small bell tower and semi-circular opening in the pediment of the portico. The doorway on the portico comes from the 1928 renovation.

The county seat named Taylorsville for George Taylor, a hero of the American Revolution, but throughout the history of the county the site of government was Patrick Court House. In 1884, the town was renamed Stuart in honor of Civil War General James Ewell Brown Stuart, who was born and raised in Ararat. J. E. B. Stuart's father Archibald Stuart served as Commonwealth's Attorney of Patrick County.

The most famous court case held in the building occurred in January 1878 as part of *Ex Parte Virginia*. Burwell Reynolds, age nineteen, and Lee Reynolds, age seventeen, were the children of Kitty Reynolds, who lived at the Rock Springs Farm, today the Reynolds Homestead, administered by Virginia Tech.

In the kitchen, a separate structure at the Reynolds Homestead hangs a picture of Kitty Reynolds, the slave that traditions states saved the life of Hardin Reynolds. She distracted a raging bull long enough by twirling her skirts for the father of R.

J. to escape danger, but it as a mother that she should be more famous. The Reynolds made her the nanny for their sixteen children while Kittie, born in 1838, had eighteen or more children herself.

After the Civil War, Kittie became a midwife in Patrick County she still called home. The Reynolds Family never forgot her. Here are two stories that tell of that appreciation.

On November 29, 1877, at the end of Reconstruction after the Civil War, the Reynolds brothers got into a fight with the white brothers Green and Aaron Shelton near the present-day site of the Patrick County School's bus maintenance garage. The cause of the altercation was verbal harassment by the Shelton boys directed at a school for former slaves at the site overlooking Campbell's Branch.

Aaron Shelton knocked Lee Reynolds over a log near the road, and Burwell stabbed Shelton with a knife resulting in Shelton's death the next day. In April 1878, Patrick County tried the two Reynolds brothers separately. Judge William Treadway presided and with all white juries.

Mary Reynolds Lybrook, one of the Reynolds children that Kittie helped to raise got her husband Virginia State Senator and attorney Andrew Murray Lybrook along with attorney William Martin to represent Kittie's sons. Both former Confederate officers, now lawyers, asked that the juries for the two Reynolds brothers be comprised of one-third African-American, which Judge William Treadway denied.

The court found Burwell guilty of first-degree murder after a second trial. Lee received an eighteen-year sentence for second-degree murder after a second trial.

The attorneys petitioned Judge Alexander Rives of the Federal District of Western Virginia to move the cases to federal court because the state court denied the defendant's rights due to a lack of blacks on the juries and they could not receive a fair trial in Patrick County due to their race.

On November 18, 1878, Deputy U. S. Marshall O. R. Wooten arrived in Stuart to take the Reynolds brothers under his protection. A chain of events began that ended up in the U.S. Supreme Court.

Editorials in newspapers and Resolutions in the Virginia General Assembly said Judge Rives actions were a "Federal usurpation of power" and "unwarranted by the Constitution." Virginia's Attorney General asked Congress to pass legislation to prevent Federal courts from "usurping" the power of state courts. Newspapers as far away as Baltimore and New York commented on the case that began as a senseless killing in Patrick County.

Judge Rives responded by calling two grand juries that included black men that eventually indicted judges in Amherst, Appomattox, Bedford, Botetourt, Buckingham, Campbell, Charlotte, Franklin, Fluvanna, Halifax, Henry, Nelson, and Roanoke counties. Judges charged were Judge James D. Coles of Pittsylvania County and Judge Samuel G. Staples of Patrick County. The charges included excluding African-Americans from juries violating the Civil Rights Act of 1875 and the Fourteenth Amendment to the United States Constitution, which guaranteed "equal protection of the law."

Of all the judges arrested only Judge James Doddridge Coles of Pittsylvania County refused bail and petitioned the U. S.

Supreme Court for a writ of habeas corpus claiming he had not violated any law becoming a case forever known as Ex Parte Virginia.

On March 15, 1880, the Supreme Court denied the petition, thus upholding Judge Rives actions as part of decisions on three separate cases commonly referred to as "The Civil Rights Cases" that set precedents for the protection of rights for the former slaves. The courthouse in Chatham received National Landmark status in 1987 due to this case instead of Patrick mainly because the National Park Service did not dig deep enough to find the roots of the case were in Patrick County.

Burwell Reynolds received a sentence of five years for manslaughter for killing Aaron Shelton. Patrick County did not prosecute Lee Reynolds and released him.

Further information can are in the writings of Herman Melton's *Pittsylvania County's Historic Courthouse: The Story Behind Ex Parte Virginia* and *"Thirty-Nine Lashes-Well Laid On:" Crime and Punishment in Southside Virginia 1750-1950*.

As stated earlier, the Reynolds family did not forget Kittie, the former slave, who saved the life of family patriarch Hardin Reynolds from a raging bull. Richard Joshua Reynolds had left Patrick County, Virginia, to go to nearby Winston, North Carolina. It was not Winston-Salem yet.

R. J. Reynolds made a fortune as a tobacco magnate, and his kindness to Kittie Reynolds speaks to his largess. He bought her a home and sent his chauffeur to drive a car to Patrick County to get her and bring her to his home in Winston-Salem to visit his family.

WASHINGTON, Oct. 15.—The following arguments were made in the United States Supreme Court to-day, in regard to Judge Rives's decision upholding the right of colored men to be tried by colored juries:

The murder site in Stuart, Virginia, near the school bus garage.

Dentist Hege had his office upstairs in this building on Main Street in Mount Airy, North Carolina.

Chapter Four:

<u>DEADLY DENTIST</u>

Many people are afraid to go to the dentist, but I am not one of them. For four decades, Thomas Jackson, D.D.S., P. A. has been my dentist. Every visit involves a conversation, a bit of a one-sided one as Dr. Jackson usually has his hands in my mouth. Due to tetracycline, an antibiotic taken in my youth, my teeth became darker than normal. In my twenties, Dr. Jackson came up with a way to place veneers on my top front six teeth that are still in place today. Pictures of my teeth went all over the country to dental conferences as I was the first veneer patient in North Carolina. Back to our conversations, they often were about history, his, mine, and the area we live including Mount Airy, North Carolina, and that leads to the next murder in a rearview mirror that this book explores.

Decades before the Unabomber blew his victims into the headlines, Mount Airy, North Carolina, had a reputation as "Little Chicago." Crime was not the image of the fictional Mayberry from the 1960s *The Andy Griffith Show* or the town Andy Griffith grew up in in the 1930s and 1940s. Tourists come looking for the simple life the brochures promote and not the criminal life. All that changed in 1936 in a case of murder based on the obsession one man had for a pretty girl that was once his receptionist.

Dr. Harvey Richard Hege, a local dentist, lived across the street on the corner of Cherry and South Main Streets across from where the Mount Airy Municipal Building sits today in a Spanish-Mission style home built in 1925 with his wife, Alice Williams Hege of Baltimore, Maryland.

Hege practiced dentistry in Mount Airy for twenty-five years. His office was above the F. D. Holcomb Hardware Store, where the Main Oak Emporium occupies today in the Midkiff Building, which was a hardware store in the building that bears their name. Hege took over for Dr. R. W. Reece and at the time of the crime was working with a lab in Hillsville on experimental new material for artificial dentures. The son of J. A. Hege of Friedburg, North Carolina, near Winston-Salem in Forsyth County, Hege received his education at Maryland Dental College. He had three sisters, who married Misters Talley and Boyles of Winston-Salem and a Mister Burkhead of Charlotte.

Elsie Dickerson Salmons Thomas described as "pretty enough to make you forget about going to the dentist" was Dr. Hege's receptionist for three years until she met and married Curry Thomas of Cape Charles, Virginia, a small town on the west coast of the Eastern Shore of Virginia. Today, you can get there across the Chesapeake Bay Bridge from Virginia Beach, but then it was accessed by ferry. Elsie's brother W. A. Dickerson lived in Cape Charles, and that is how she met her future husband.

She contemplated leaving Dr. Hege's employment earlier due to his "infatuation" with her. Hege wrote Elsie letters "strongly" objecting to her leaving to get married. Elsie left Mount Airy on June 10 to marry Curry Thomas in Hillsville at her mother's home. Dr. Hege was obsessed with Elsie. He sent her telegrams after she left his employment telling her ominously that if he could not have her, no one would.

After a honeymoon, the couple began their lives in Cape Charles. Married only a month upon arriving at the post office on Wednesday, July 22, 1936, after playing golf, Curry and Elsie Thomas discovered a package wrapped in paper and tied up with a string with a Richmond, Virginia, postmark. The couple thought it was a wedding present from the groom's father and decided not to open the package until they returned home. Employees at the post office encouraged them to open the package there, but Thomas refusing saved their lives.

They arrived at their new home, The Hermitage, built before 1783, was a mile east of Cape Charles. The home framed by shade trees and surrounded by a white wooden fence looked out over King's Creek. Curry Thomas picked up the package and placed it in his lap and began to open the package.

Elsie opened the car door and stepped onto the running board at which time she heard a click, a sharp click, and everything went black for her. The blast knocked Elsie out of the car, and she lay unconscious on the ground. Field hands on the farm found her as car parts were still raining down on the yard.

She deliriously repeated, "It looks like a mousetrap." The bomb injured her left arm and left eye. She was age 35 at the time of the bombing.

Her husband did not fare so well. Curry Thomas, age 47, was blown up and out of the roof of the car by the blast. His body, so badly mutilated, mad identification impossible. His watch stopped at 6:17 p.m. The blast blew car parts over one hundred yards from the vehicle. Citizens of Cape Charles heard the blast over a mile away.

It was both Curry and Elsie's second marriages. Her first to John Salmons of nearby Galax, Virginia, ended after three years. Newspapers described John this way. "People of Galax and Hillsville who know him feel confident he has no connection with the crime." Two years earlier, John received a fractured skull in a fight in Hillsville and suffered from a "partial loss of his mind" and spent time in the mental hospital in Marion, Virginia. Officials cleared John Salmons of any wrongdoing in the bomb that injured his ex-wife and killed her second husband. Curry Thomas had lost his first wife in a train wreck before he met Elsie.

Dr. Harvey Hege, age 47, and a friend from Mount Airy, Ed

Banner, age 52, were fishing at Fisherman's Ferry on the New

River hundreds of miles away. Banner, a Work Progress

Administration timekeeper, came from the family that

Bannertown near Mount Airy got its name.

They laid Curry Thomas to rest on Friday, July 24, 1936,

while his wife recovered at a hospital in nearby Nassawadox,

Virginia. Cape Charles Postmaster S. Thomas Nottingham notified

federal authorities when he realized it was a mail bomb that killed

Curry Thomas and injured Elsie beginning a three-month

investigation that resulted in two arrests and one more death.

Investigators flew in from Baltimore, Maryland. Standing

six feet and weighing two hundred and fifty pounds, B. B. Webb

was joined by "a little mustache fellow," J. B. Sentman.

Described as "Mutt and Jeff," they began their

investigation at the scene of the crime, where they found a label

from the battery that powered the device and a piece of the

mailing label. The bomb had a mouse trap like device that

triggered the bomb when opened. After four days investigating on the Eastern Shore, officials turned their eyes west and north to follow leads.

By July 28, joined by another Postal Inspector named Bleakly, Webb, and Sentman were in Mount Airy, North Carolina, interested in Elsie's brother Jesse Dickerson and Dr. Hege. They asked questions at Midkiff's Hardware and Houston Creasy's Plumbing company.

The "C" battery led to a company in Canada that manufactured the product and sold it to a Cleveland, Ohio, company that shipped a specific batch to northwest North Carolina, which led to a hardware store in Mount Airy. Dr. Hege purchased dynamite and plumbing materials including two pipe caps and a two-inch pipe nipple from Creasy's Plumbing in Mount Airy two weeks before the explosion. Investigators even traced the type of string that wrapped the package to Dr. Hege.

The mailing address, produced on a typewriter manufactured in Chicago, Illinois, led to a typewriter sitting on the desk of Dr. Hege in Mount Airy. Typewriters, like a human being's fingerprints, leave a unique pattern.

Witnesses placed Dr. Hege and his friend, Ed Banner, in Richmond, on the day the package was mailed. The noose was closing in on the two suspects, and a trick on the two would lead to their arrest.

Federal District Attorney Sterling Hutcheson along with Virginia State Police along with Commonwealth Attorney C. M. Lankford, Jr. and Sheriff George Turner of Northampton County, Virginia, among others worked together across jurisdictions to trap the suspects. Postal inspectors J. R. Sentman of Wilmington, Delaware, R. R. Webb, and G. J. Bleakley of Richmond worked with local officials such as Jake Earing of Martinsville, Virginia, and J. R. Richardson of Galax.

The plan was simple, a woman, a "decoy," known only to the officers would lure Hege and Banner out of North Carolina up to Galax, Virginia so that working with North Carolina officials would not be necessary and arrest them in Virginia. On Monday, October 5, 1936, Hege and Banner rode up the Low Gap Road, now Highway 89 in a Plymouth owned by the dentist with a "strange woman." The "unsuspecting prisoners" entered the lobby of the Bluemont Hotel around 10 p.m., no doubt thinking of romantic entanglements, but instead, Sheriff Turner arrested and handcuffed them.

After their arrest, Dr. Hege and Ed Banner rode the 350 miles across Virginia to Cape Charles arriving at the ferry to cross the Chesapeake Bay at 7 a.m. on Tuesday, October 6, 1936. Hege summoned Mount Airy attorneys Edward G. Webb and John H. Folger, who came to the Eastern Shore with Hege's wife.

That evening, Hege attempted suicide. Deputy John R. Womble foiled the attempt when he discovered blood seeping from Hege's cell. Hege claimed it was an accident that he cut himself on his wristwatch, but Hege carried a pocket watch. Dr. Holland Trower stitched up the dentist.

On Saturday, Hege asked for his glasses to read the papers surrounding his case without getting a headache. He claimed, "I may have been indiscreet, but as God is my witness, I had nothing to do with that bomb." That evening Hege proceeded to cut a wrist and jugular vein. He bled into an open suitcase to prevent discovery. A jail orderly, Robert Truitt found Hege dead on Sunday morning around 6 a.m. He had been dead about an hour, and authorities found no suicide note. He was dead before his wife and lawyers arrived back in Mount Airy, where Hege would soon follow.

Ed Banner remained in custody a little longer, but three weeks after Hege's suicide, he returned home to Mount Airy with no charges pending against him. He claimed Hege told him they went to Richmond to check on Mrs. Hege, whom the dentist suspected of having an affair. Hege told Banner not to discuss the trip to anyone.

Dr. Hege was laid to rest at the Grace Moravian Cemetery on Wednesday, October 14, 1936, on the three acres of land he donated. Reverend C. D. Crouch presided over the service. It would be this same church that Andy Griffith made his way to a dozen years later to learn to play the trombone because the Moravians had a brass band that his church, Haymore Baptist Church, did not.

The Federal authorities closed the case on November 8, 1936. Three years later, Congress voted monetary rewards to three persons who helped solve the case. In 1941, True Detective Magazine did a story about the Mount Airy Mail Bomber.

Elsie left the hospital on October 20, 1936, and recovered in time. She later remarried and moved to Amarillo, Texas, where she died in 1961.

The home of Curry and Elsie Thomas, where the bomb exploded.

The driveway of the Thomas home, where the bomb exploded.

The grave of Curry Thomas, who lost his life in the explosion.

The home of Curry Thomas, where the explosion occurred.

Newspaper story documenting the bomb explosion.

Elsie Thomas survived the explosion that took her husband's life.

Curry Thomas lost his life in the bomb explosion.

Dr. Hege's grave at Grace Moravian Church in Mount Airy. He donated the land and was the first grave in the cemetery.

Dental chair in the collection of the Mount Airy Museum of Regional History that may have belonged to Dr. Hege.

Chair in the collection of the Mount Airy Museum of Regional History that belonged to Dr. Hege.

U. OF MD. GIVES UP

IN BRIEF

THE AFRO AMERICAN

28 Pages — **NATIONAL EDITION**

BALTIMORE, MD., FEBRUARY 10, 1951

HOTEL SNOOTY, SOCIAL WORKERS CANCEL MEETING; WAR HERO WINS 'LOYALTY' FIGHT

DOOMED 7 CALM TO END

Univ. of Md. Board Opens School to All

Admits Its 'Makeshift Policies' Have Been Unfair and Illegal

BALTIMORE

Kidnaping Is Called Hoax

Free N.C. Man Who Cut Cop

How Martinsville 7 Were Put to Death

Mass Execution Ends Martinsville Case

Governor Says Communists Did Not Influence Him to Deny Clemency

War Hero Wins Loyalty Fight

Social Workers Cancel Meeting; Hotel Snooty

U.S. Artillery Stupifies Reds

Ohio Air Crash Deals Survivors Twin Blows

AS 3 ROTC PROFESSORS DIE!

Marshall Heads for Korean Front

INSIDE YOUR AFRO

Stay Out of Birmingham or Give It to the Mexicans

DEAL BLOW TO SEGREGATION:

94

Chapter Five:

THE MARTINSVILLE SEVEN

The story you are about to read seems impossible to believe in 2017, not because the men in question committed the crime described, but they all lost their lives. This story is about rape crossing color lines and the criminal justice system. Some might say today it shows a lack of social justice condemning a group of seven men because they were not the same color as the victim. They were African-Americans living in the South before the dawn of the Civil Rights Movement. These men deserved punishment, but they deserved fair punishment without their skin color being the deciding factor.

White men that committed the same crime did not lose their lives. Other states such as Texas, Georgia, and North Carolina also executed Black men for rape. One of the attorneys for the men in this story once stated that "We don't need to lynch. We can try them and then hang them."

I am a firm believer that you should not pass judgment on someone in the past by applying our modern-day views upon them. They lived in a different time, and one person could not overturn an entire system now or then. Men who fought for the Confederacy are racist by today's standards, but in their time, they lived in a system where slavery was legal and even endorsed by many religious leaders.

That is not to say that we cannot hold the system they lived under, whether economic or legal, as abhorrent to our beliefs today. You should never judge a person unless you can walk a mile in their shoes and we cannot do that today comparing to people in the 1860s or the 1950s. We hope that our nation will progress until all people are equal under the law and in the hearts of their fellow countrymen.

From 1600 until 1949, 588 Black men lost their lives as the penalty for rape in southern states of the United States. During that same period, only 48 White men received the same penalty. This case is interesting for other historical reasons as it is one of the first cases to use statistics to prove discrimination.

This story also reflects another gap in race relations. People like to place everyone in convenient categories assuming that all people of the same race agree on the same issue. This case shows that not to be true as the leadership of the National Association for the Advancement of Colored People (NAACP) and the Civil Rights Congress (CRC) did not agree about the legal strategy surrounding the men in this case.

In 1791, Martinsville, Virginia, got its start when George Hairston, one of the richest and largest slave owners in the nation at the time, donated fifty acres in the city named for Revolutionary War hero Joseph Martin. The courthouse, built in 1824, where this case was tried sits on this tract of land and is today an historical museum for the Martinsville Henry County Historical Society. The county and eastern namesake county gave Patrick Henry his name on Virginia maps, and his portrait still hangs in the courtroom. It is a building where the 1901 statue honoring Confederate Soldiers still sits on the grounds of the building.

After World War Two, Martinsville and Henry County became a booming region beginning from the agriculture including tobacco to the furniture of Bassett, the mills of Fieldcrest, and other textiles such as Pannill Knitting Company to the largest employer, DuPont. Unemployment in the area was almost non-existent.

Today, what use to be a spur line of the Danville and Western Railroad makes its way from the main that cuts through the middle of Martinsville, Virginia. It is a walking trail as is the main line that adds much to the community, but in 1949 it was the scene of one of the most infamous crimes in the history of the once boomtown in Southside Virginia.

On January 8, 1949, a 32-year-old white woman named Ruby Floyd knocked on the door of Mrs. Mary Wade around 7:30 p.m. When Mrs. Wade opened the door, she found Ruby Floyd standing in her doorway. Floyd told Wade that a group of seven black men had gang-raped her. She claimed at first that two waves of men attacked her, but she escaped, but they dragged her back where other men joined in the crime. She claimed she encountered a woman during her short escape, who did nothing to help her and then the men caught her and dragged her back. Floyd cried as she told the story. She had bruises on her elbows, forearms, knees, lower legs, and thighs. Muddy, she wore a torn slip with no underwear or skirt. She carried a coat and dress that were extremely dirty. She had a swollen lip, scratches on her neck, chest, and buttocks. Mr. Wade got his gun and took Ruby to a nearby store to call the police.

Floyd told the police she recognized two of her attackers walking down the street. Police promptly arrested them. These two men confessed to the crime, and Police arrested five other men. They became the Martinsville Seven, a group of men who lost their lives and became a cause for many groups, but it was 1949, several years before the Civil Rights Movement of the 1950s started a wave that would make their executions impossible several years later.

Ruby Floyd moved to Martinsville, Virginia, in 1945, so her husband, Glenn Floyd, could run United Dollar Department Store. A devoted Jehovah's Witness, Ruby Floyd "proselytized" in the

Black community. That evening she was looking to collect a "small debt" and felt comfortable walking alone due to her previous experience spreading the word of God. Ruth Pettie owed Ruby Floyd $6 for clothing including a second-hand suit and shoes.

It was a Saturday night when Ruby knocked on Nannie Gilmer's door searching for Ruth Pettie. Gilmer warned Ruby not to go but sent eleven-year-old Charlie Martin, the son of Rosa went with her.

Four men exited the Rex Theater. Howard Hairston pulled a pint of alcohol for a drink. He stopped by the liquor store and got two more bottles. Several of the men including Frank Hairston and Booker T. Millner drank under the water tower along the Danville and Western Railroad. Joe Henry Hairston saw Ruby and Charlie coming and initiated the contact with her.

Francis DeSales Grayson burst into the home of Ethel Mae Redd announcing that some boys had a lady upon the railroad tracks. Grayson, who was married with five children, lived with Redd.

Multiple people were in the vicinity walking along the railroad tracks including Grayson's wife, Josephine, who was going to catch a bus for a trip to the doctor. Leola Millner, sister of Booker T. Millner, was another. John Travis Redd was headed to a movie.

Ruby Floyd appeared asking for help. She clung to Mrs. Grayson. Joe Henry Hampton pulled her away. Three more men Frank and Howard Hairston along with Booker Millner joined the other men making it seven in total.

At 7:15 p.m. Ruby Floyd knocked on the door of Jesse and Mary Wade. She wore a torn slip with tangled hair, laced with pine needles. Her arms were scratched, and her thighs were red. Her clothes including a shirt and sweater were muddy, and she had multiple bruises on her arms and legs.

The Wades walked Floyd to the paint shop owned by Martinsville Mayor Nick Prillaman. At 8:15 p.m. Police Car #3 with Officers T. G. Finney and R. L. Stover arrived, followed soon by Sgt. Murray V. Barrow and a detective. Ruby took Barrow to the crime scene, which was a half mile away along the railroad to the east of the right away. On their return to the paint store, Floyd

recognized Booker T. Millner and Frank Hairston walking by and

identified them as two of her attackers. Officers Finney and Stover

took the two into custody. Barrow took Ruby Floyd to the

hospital.

Frank Hairston, age 18, at the time of the crime bragged to

Finney about "getting me a little piece." He worked several jobs

after leaving school in the seventh grade such as at Woolworth's,

lumber, and tobacco.

Booker T. Millner, age 19, at the time of the crime, quit

school in the eleventh grade. Arrested once before in 1947 for

drinking, he worked at a local cemetery.

Medical exams confirmed that Floyd was the victim of

multiple sexual assaults. She screamed during the exam and

doctors sedated her. Like many victims of rape, she endured years

of physical and emotional issues related to the crime.

Barrow returned from the hospital to question Millner and Frank Hairston. He called the Virginia State Police, and James H. Barnes arrived around ten o'clock.

At 1:45 a.m. Frank Hairston confessed to Barnes and implicated Frank Hairston, Booker Millner, Howard Hairston, and Joe Henry Hampton saying the latter started the encounter. Police arrested other men implicated, and another turned himself into authorities after talking to Mrs. Wade. All seven eventually confessed to the crime.

Officer Finney found four defendants sleeping at home. Arrested twice before, John Clabon Taylor, age 21, had a fourth-grade education and worked at Virginia Beach.

James Luther Hairston, age 20, worked in tobacco and furniture. Police questioned he and Taylor. By 4:30 a.m. he signed a statement implicating the other men.

Howard Lee Hairston, age 18, was half-brother to another suspect. Never arrested, he lived with his Aunt Irene Hodge. When told of the other confessions, he made a statement claiming impotence, but thereby implicated himself.

At 5:30 a.m., Barnes interrogated Francis DeSales Grayson, age 37, an Army Veteran in World War II, who was married with five children. Never arrested and from Maryland, Grayson had lived in North Carolina and New Jersey. He claimed to have been walking along railroad tracks when he heard Ruby begging for help. He got James Hairston and John C. Taylor and returned to the scene with the other four. He claimed he was the last one to join in and was impotent, no doubt due to alcohol, a common defense for several of the seven men.

As the sun came up over Martinsville, officials became concerned over the safety of the six suspects in custody fearing a lynch mob or vigilante justice coming down on the men accused of raping a white woman. They moved them to the jail in nearby Stuart, Virginia, the county seat of Patrick. They arrived at 7:30 a.m.

Barrow returned to the crime scene, finding the spot about fifty yards from the tracks in a low gully in the woods. He discovered a felt hat and an earring. Ruby Floyd returned to the hospital because of the attack on her. She later went to Duke University Hospital with continuing health problems.

Word was getting around Martinsville that morning. Betty Underwood Nickelston was to babysit her nephew Eddie Underwood that day. Her sister-in-law, Ruby Underwood, made her husband meet his sister at the train station as she arrived from Ferrum, where she lived in Franklin County, and walk her to the house.

Police were still searching for Joe Henry Hampton. Hampton, age 19, moved to Henry County in 1943 with a reputation for trouble. At 17, he received a conviction for grand larceny, followed by probation issues and trouble holding a job. On Monday morning, after sleeping in the woods all weekend, he came to Mrs. Wade's house, where she persuaded him to surrender on her front porch about 9 a.m. to Barrow and two officers.

Hampton told Barrow that he Millner, Howard Hairston, and Frank Hairston were drinking wine as Ruby Floyd approached them. He said she "put up a big scuffle" refuting claims that she consented.

One article quotes the interrogation of young Charlie Martin saying law enforcement told him, "Charlie, do you know what happens to little boys who tell lies then they die?" Martin replied, "Yes sir. They go to hell." Millner gave Martin a quarter to keep his name out of it.

Their stories confirmed that four of the men were drinking when they saw Floyd with the Martin boy. These were Howard Hairston, Frank Hairston, Booker T. Millner, and Joe Henry Hampton. "We all planned to get her when she came back." They chased, subdued her, and sent Charlie Martin home. Another went to a house and told other men they had a woman near the railroad tracks. This man returned with two others, and they all joined in on the sexual assault. These three men were Francis DeSales Grayson, John Clabon Taylor, and James Luther Hairston.

Grayson, a married man, was the eldest in his thirties with five children urged the other two Taylor and James Hairston to join him in the crime. The other men were in their late teens, or early twenties were laborers. They were not well educated and still lived with their families, but it was noted nothing in their past indicated that they were capable of this level of violence or raping a woman. Six were single men, and all were employed, three in a sawmill, one a plasterer, one a stone cutter, and one a foundryman.

Several witnesses backed up Floyd's story. She needed directions to the home of the person, who owed her money. One family offered their eleven-year-old son, Charlie Martin, as a guide, who saw the first group grab Floyd. The family had warned Floyd not to come back after dark. They sent him away giving him a quarter and a knife. He was the witness that led to the first confession.

Mrs. Ethel Mae Redd told that Grayson lodged with her and that he urged the other two Taylor and James Hairston to return with him. Three other people confirmed Ruby Floyd's escape. One was Leona Millner, sister of Booker T. Millner, one of the accused. Another was Josephine Grayson, wife of Francis

Grayson. Reportedly, Ruby Floyd tore off a button from her coat while trying to escape.

Officials geographically separated the seven men with two in Stuart, one in Chatham, the county seat of Pittsylvania County and four in Roanoke. This action prevented any local lynch mobs from trying to take justice into their own hands.

A preliminary hearing in front of Judge M. H. MacBryde moved from the Martinsville City Hall to the Henry County Court House along with a time change with no public notice to protect the suspects from the possibility of retaliation. Seventeen law enforcement officers were guarding the Martinsville Seven in the courtroom. There was no bail for the men.

The only criticism of law enforcement came from *The Daily Worker,* a publication of the Communist Party. Law enforcement showed a restrained behavior and the safety of the men was a constant point of focus. While Virginia might punish the men, the public at large would not act as judge and jury.

The court case began on April 19, 1949, when Judge Kennon C. Whittle of Martinsville met with lawyers for the seven men, whom he appointed separately for each man on January 22. Frank Burton of Stuart, a state legislator, who was not a "champion of Civil Rights," was a Dixiecrat in 1948 supporting Strom Thurmond for President, represented John C. Taylor. William L. Joyce of Stuart, "one of the foremost defense attorneys," represented DeSales Grayson. Joseph C. Whitehead, Jr., the former Commonwealth Attorney of Henry County represented Joe Henry Hampton. William F. Carter represented Frank Hairston. Claude E. Taylor, Jr., who had been practicing law less than a year, represented Booker Millner. Clarence Kearfott represented James Hairston. Stephen D. Martin represented Howard Hairston. The lawyers received $25 for three months work.

Commonwealth Attorney Irvin W. Cubine prosecuted the case for Virginia. Cubine, age 48, began practicing law in 1929, which included three years as City Attorney for Martinsville and beginning in 1942 Commonwealth Attorney for Henry County. He had two assistants including W. R. Broaddus, Jr., a member of the Virginia House of Delegates beginning in 1946 and the chief prosecutor of the county for eighteen years. Hannibal N. Joyce, a former law partner of Judge Whittle, who had been Commonwealth Attorney for Henry County for ten years, was the other assistant to Cubine. All three men were very connected in the business community of Martinsville and Henry County.

Judge Whittle, age 57 at the time of the trial. Described as "A worthy son of a noble sire," he was born in 1891 and grew up at Athol on Church Street in Martinsville. The son of Judge Stafford G. Whittle, who was a judge of the Virginia Supreme Court of Appeals from 1901 until 1919. Kennon graduated from Washington and Lee College and went to the University of Virginia for law school. He served on the U. S. District Court for Western Virginia from 1922-26. He was a delegate for the 1932 Democratic National Convention that nominated Franklin Roosevelt and a year later served in a Virginia Constitutional Convention. In 1944, Kennon Whittle was elected to the 7th Judicial Circuit Court, where he never had a ruling overturned. In 1951, Governor John

S. Battle appointed him to the Virginia Supreme Court of Appeals making he and his father the only father-son combination to serve on the court.

The Grand Jury that recommended the defendants for trial had black members, but the trial jury was all white. There were blacks in the jury pool, but they were "struck" due to their opposition to the death penalty "without comment" by the prosecution. The 72 selected jurors were all white.

Judge Whittle warned the attorneys not to mention race during the trial, and he separated the cases individually except for one when two defendants asked to be tried together. Whittle warned the attorneys that "propriety and decorum" would be observed and that the defendants would receive a "fair and impartial trial" in his courtroom. He encouraged them to "downplay racial overtones for community stability" as Martinsville and Henry County had "a negro population of splendid citizens...It must be tried as though both parties were members of the same race. I will not have it otherwise."

There were calls to move the trials, but prominent Black leaders such as Dr. Dana O. Baldwin, famous today for the Baldwin Block on Fayette Street, opposed moving it. He came from Philadelphia, Pennsylvania, in 1910, and was the first Black doctor in the county. He invested in businesses that included a shopping center, hotel, and a twelve-room hospital. His success had not created "any strained relationship between the races." Judge Whittle denied any attempts to move the trials.

There were local Black organizations including members of the NAACP and the Colored Knights of Pythias Lodge found Martinsville "surprisingly harmonious." *The Martinsville Bulletin* stirred the pot using "highly inflammatory" language voicing concerns about a fair jury.

Since the trials were separate, Virginia had to prove the guilt of each defendant and could not use the confessions of the other defendants as evidence. Each defendant received one count of rape and six counts of aiding and abetting rape.

Trials began on April 21, 1949, with Joe Henry Hampton going first as the prosecution considered him as the "ringleader."

They had the strongest case against him as he had a criminal record and had avoided capture initially. Next came Frank Hairston, Booker Millner, and Howard Hairston. The last three being for James Hairston, John Taylor, and DeSales Grayson.

Ruby Floyd had to testify multiple times. There were some discrepancies such as different numbers of attackers, and she could not identify them all due to darkness. She said she did not scream as there was a murder threat. Judge Whittle did not allow any comments on her judgment on being there on a Saturday night. The Judge lost patience with an attorney at preliminary questioned Floyd's calmness. They were not going to have the victim placed on trial. She said she could not run due to her injuries.

During the trials, several defendants claimed they were drunk or that Floyd consented to sex. As is the case today in many rape trials, the victim received harsh treatment at the hands of the defense lawyers. Many locals blamed her for being in the wrong area of town at the wrong time pointing out several black ladies warned her not to be around by herself at that time of day.

Ruby Floyd said that Hampton blocked her path and grabbed her from behind. The men threw her down near the tracks and took turns holding her down. She said Hampton "penetrated" her more than once and threatened to kill her, slapped her, and covered her mouth. She escaped at one point and met a man, John Redd, a woman, Josephine Grayson, the wife of one of her attackers, who was more worried about getting her clothes dirty than helping Ruby, and a teenage girl, Leola Millner, Booker's 14-year-old sister, along the railroad tracks.

The men drug Floyd back to the gully in the woods and had sex with her 12 to 14 times including sodomizing her. She sobbed "violently" in several of the trials and said the attack "paralyzed" her from the hips down.

The defense lawyers questioned her ability to identify her attackers and pointed out Ruby received warnings about being out alone that night. Some of the attorneys did not question her at all. They tried to use their clients' youth and use of alcohol as an excuse for their behavior. The first four claimed they spent most of that Saturday afternoon drinking. Four of the defendants testified including Hampton, Millner, James Hairston, and Frank

Hairston. Some of them claimed they did not aid the others or

that Ruby had not resisted, so it could not be rape or that they

paid her for sex. Several of the defendants asked for mercy or

repudiated their confessions. There were several character

witnesses called to aid the defendants.

The prosecution called Mary Wade to the stand after Ruby

to confirm Hampton's admission to her before his surrender to

authorities. Ethel Mae Redd connected the last three men on trial

to the events. Little Charlie Martin put the first four at the scene.

Law enforcement testified next in the trials. Then the doctors

came forward including Dr. Baynard Carter of Duke commenting

that the attack was so violent that it took Ruby six to nine months

to recover.

There were six trials in eleven days and seven convictions.

Four of the seven testified in the trials, and one claimed he did

not have intercourse with Floyd. All deliberations by the all-white

juries were under two hours, and all seven received the death penalty. Blacks in Martinsville were reportedly "shocked" over the severity of the sentences.

This case received national attention. The National Association for the Advancement of Colored People (NAACP) worked through the court system to reduce the death penalty. They accepted the guilt of the defendants. They used the law firm of Hill, Martin, and Robinson, all graduates of Howard University like Thurgood Marshall of the NAACP. Attorney Martin W. Martin of Danville, a prominent African-American, argued the venue of the trials should have been changed and that the trials should not have taken place serially. The fact that the juries were composed exclusively of those for the death penalty doomed the defendants. They argued that the death penalty for rape was "reserved for blacks." Other civil rights attorneys included Samuel W. Tucker, Roland D. Ealey, Oliver W. Hill, and others. The attorneys used statistical, historical, and sociological methods of legal arguments in the appeal process.

The NAACP, which began in 1909, focused on lobbying, education, publicity, and a magazine called Crisis, edited by W. E.

B. DuBois, who opposed the emphasis on legal action. The group had one legal counsel beginning in 1938, who would become the first African-American to serve on the U. S. Supreme Court, Thurgood Marshall.

Another group, the Civil Rights Congress, focused on the racial issues of the case. They demonstrated, wrote letters, worked for media attention outside Virginia. The group, known for Communist sympathies, did not sit well with those in Virginia in the early 1950s. The Emmett Till case was another they were involved with including several "red cases," which involved the suppression of suspected Communist Party members. The CRC began in 1946 when several organizations came together. While there was no Communist Party affiliation, many of the leadership of the organization were Communist.

The CRC and NAACP conflicted throughout the appeal process. While the latter focused on the legal access, the CRC wanted to protest and take direct action. There was little cooperation between the two organizations. It seemed to some that the two organizations were more interested in who represented the Martinsville Seven instead of their fates.

The Virginia and local NAACP focused on the issue of a fair trial and not whether the Seven were guilty. The reason for this is clear when you look at the history of rape in Virginia.

From 1626 when records begin through 1908, three whites and 99 blacks were hung for rape. Until 1866, only blacks got death by state law. In 1866, a law change applied death to both races, but no whites were executed for rape. In 1908, Virginia became the fifth state to take control of execution from local authority via the electric chair at the Richmond Penitentiary. From that time, up to the time of the "Martinsville Seven," 45 black men were executed for rape, and another eight received the sentence of death. During that time, only one white man received the death penalty, and he was pardoned. In Virginia, blacks were executed twice as many times as white men, who received life sentences. In the entire southern states between 1938-43, 93% of men executed for rape were black.

This was not equal protection under the law. Martin filed a writ of habeas corpus saying the defendants were denied equal protection under the Fourteenth Amendment.

Section One of the Fourteenth Amendment to the United States Constitution passed in 1868 after the Civil War states the following. *"All persons born or naturalized in the United States, and subject to the jurisdiction thereof, are citizens of the United States and of the State wherein they reside. No State shall make or enforce any law which shall abridge the privileges or immunities of citizens of the United States; nor shall any State deprive any person of life, liberty, or property, without due process of law; nor deny to any person within its jurisdiction the equal protection of the laws."*

There is the rub for the seven men from Martinsville. Their race condemned them to the electric chair. Their cases rose through the appeals process. First, in the "Hustings Court," which held jurisdiction in Richmond, Virginia, the state capital, where the men were imprisoned. This case was the first-time statistics were used in a racial challenge to the death penalty.

Virginia Attorney General and future Governor J. Lindsay Almond used the due process argument stating that the legal process was followed in the case. The key line from amendment states, "No person shall ... be deprived of life, liberty, or property, without due process of law..." Almond argued that the seven men had received due process and were guilty and ignored the equal protection aspects of the case.

The Fifth Amendment to the United States Constitution says the following. "No person shall be held to answer for a capital, or otherwise infamous crime, unless on a presentment or indictment of a grand jury, except in cases arising in the land or naval forces, or in the militia, when in actual service in time of war or public danger; nor shall any person be subject for the same offense to be twice put in jeopardy of life or limb; nor shall be compelled in any criminal case to be a witness against himself, nor be deprived of life, liberty, or property, without due process of law; nor shall private property be taken for public use, without just compensation."

Judge Whittle pronounced sentence on May 3, 1949, after Grayson, Taylor, and Millner spoke. The execution was set for July 15 for the first four and July 22 for the next three. They were given sixty days to "exhaust" their appeals. Whittle complimented the prosecution. On May 4 at 11:30 a.m. with a large crowd present, the Martinsville Seven were transferred to the Virginia State Penitentiary in Richmond.

Harold Woodruff of Danville believed the defense "contested every inch of legal ground," while the *Daily Worker* called it a "Scandalous" defense. Eric Rise in the only book about the Martinsville Seven said the "quality of the defense varied widely from one attorney to another."

The silence in Martinsville was and is still amazing. E. A. Sale told Governor William Tuck that "during the trial, anyone walking by the courthouse would not have realized the trial was going on." *The Danville Bee* newspaper called the trail "a fine example of orderly justice."

On July 24, 1950, attorneys sent a clemency petition to Governor William M. Tuck, who stayed the executions until

September to allow the appeals process to proceed. He did not believe there was enough time to review the 1,000 typed pages of transcripts from the multiple trials. Tuck stated, "No fair-minded person can read the evidence in these cases without being convinced beyond the shadow of a doubt, of the guilt of all the defendants." He believed the confessions were not coerced. The Judge ruled for a "legislative response," which put the case in the hands of the governor stating they saw "no evidence that discrimination was involved." The Governor heard direct appeals on the cases against the "Martinsville Seven," but refused to intervene on their behalf. He stated he tried to save the younger men from death but felt that all seven were guilty.

A massive letter writing campaign focused on the Governor with both sides expressing their opinion to him. A fund-raising drive began for the Martinsville Seven too.

On August 26, 1949, a writ of error was sent to the Virginia Supreme Court of Appeals with arguments to be presented in January 1950. Virginia Attorney General and J. Lindsay Almond presented Virginia's case.

The Virginia Supreme Court of Appeals rejected the "racial prejudice claim" in a unanimous opinion stated that was not race of the accused, but "the circumstances, aggravation, and enormity of the crime proven in each case...one can hardly conceive of a more atrocious, a more beastly crime." The opinion came down on March 13, 1950.

On April 12, 1950, Judge Whittle set new execution dates for May 26 and June 2, respectively. Governor John S. Battle, who took office on January 18, 1950, was asked to stay the executions as the Supreme Court of the United States did not meet until May 29. On May 22, the Martinsville Seven received sixty days. Battle was accused of cultivating the "Black Vote."

On June 3, 1950, the Supreme Court met reviewing 94 of the 1,033 petitions presented. Two days later they declined to take on the case feeling that the trial was fair.

The Danville Register newspaper stated, "the seven condemned Negro rapists of Martinsville have been given the full protection of rights every human is guaranteed under the Constitution of Virginia and the United States... Virginia's reputation for justice to all its people to be…placed under a cloud."

Attorney Martin A. Martin appealed to the Federal Courts, but the U. S. Supreme Court refused to take the case. Martin started over in Federal Court, but the District Court denied the appeal and the U. S. Circuit Court refused to hear the case.

The next attempt to save the Martinsville Seven was to ask Governor Battle to give them clemency on June 23. Josephine Grayson toured Virginia with help from the CRC. There were airport demonstrations and even a rally at Madison Square Garden in New York City. There were demands that President Harry S. Truman "take moral responsibility for the lives of the Martinsville Seven" including large letter writing campaigns.

Four of the Seven wrote Governor Battle personally including Joe Hampton, who professed religious faith. Booker Millner also used religion to ask for clemency. Frank Hairston expressed he could help someone who is traveling down the same bad path as he had done. DeSales Grayson asked on behalf of his wife and five children stating he had been a "working man all my life and has been honest."

Battle promised to give the matter "serious attention" including a clemency hearing to be held on July 7, 1950. Battle was part of the Byrd political machine. He said he found no errors in the trial, while twenty-one people spoke for the Seven.

On July 21, a rally occurred in Richmond hoping to influence the Governor, but three days later he denied clemency. He commented that race had been injected and that he had been "flooded with communications of a different type" claiming innocence. Saying he had searched the records and that his conscience could not agree with claims of innocence.

The NAACP filed a Writ of Habeas Corpus claiming the Seven were denied equal protection under the 14th Amendment to the U. S. Constitution. On July 26, 1950, the day before the scheduled executions, a judge stayed the sentences until a court could hear arguments on September 30, 1950, before Judge Doubles with Virginia Attorney General J. Lindsay Almond representing the Commonwealth.

Lawyers again argued that death for Blacks in the hearing citing *Plessy v. Ferguson* from 1896 stating it "rendered the equal protection clause impotent." They hoped the appeal might go on for another two years. Thurgood Marshall was going after the "Separate, but equal" clause that he would successfully win in *Brown v. Board of Education* in 1954 over the Topeka, Kansas, school case. One argument used in defense pointed out that in 1939 only one White man was sentenced to death and his sentence was commuted, and he was pardoned. Judge Doubles denied the petition and commended Judge Whittle for the "exemplary manner in which he presided over and supervised the conduct of the cases."

On October 19, another appeal went to the Virginia Supreme Court of Appeals. Judge Whittle rescheduled the executions for November 17 and 20, 1950. On November 10, Governor Battle granted a "final stay" for 75 days so that the Seven men could have the "opportunity to assert any legal right they may have."

During the last week of November, attorneys petitioned the United States Supreme Court again. On December 29, 1950, the Supreme Court of the United States met in conference and on January 2, 1951, they denied the writ.

The political situation was now fully engaged. Governor Battle could not be seen bowing to pressure from the Communists. The NAACP "did not conform to judiciary conception of the proper method of legal argument." The Virginia and Supreme Court did not wish to have social reform. The courts were not going "to second guess juries or legislatures to put equal protection or due process above criminal law."

On January 22, 1951, the NAACP petitioned against the Virginia rape law. The CRC continued to protest nationally and in Virginia. Battle commenting on the "false propaganda" and "dastardly lies" refused to intervene. On January 30, Judge Sterling Hutchenson refused another Writ, and the Federal Courts denied Writs in Charlottesville and Charlotte, respectively.

On Friday, February 2, 1951, just after midnight, U. S. Chief Justice Fred M. Vinson personally heard the case for ninety minutes but rejected the appeal. That same night people gathered at the Richmond Penitentiary on Spring Street to pray along with 75 people praying at the Virginia Capital

At dawn of February 3, 1951, Virginia executed four of the "Martinsville Seven" via Virginia's "Electric Chair." The first was Hampton, who at age 21 went in the chair at 8:04 a.m. and was dead by 8:12 a.m. The chair housed in Building A, constructed in 1905, with the electric chair added three years later. Electrodes were placed on the head and left ankle. There were twelve witnesses present with eight from Martinsville. Next came Howard Lee Hairston at 8:32 a.m., followed by Booker T. Millner at 8:49, and finally Frank Hairston, Jr. at 9:05, who took "two jolts to die" saying "I want you all to meet me in heaven." That same day a White man, George Hailey lost his life in the chair for raping and murdering a twelve-year-old girl.

On February 4, 1951, Josephine Grayson tried to see President Harry S. Truman while 100 people protested at the White House in Washington, D. C. sponsored again by the CRC. Over 200 people marched in Richmond from Third Street Bethel

AME Church to the Capitol Square to protest the impending executions.

The three others died on Monday, February 5, 1951. John C. Taylor went at 7:41 a.m. followed by James L. Hairston at 8, who also took two jolts to die. Grayson was the last at age 38 when he died at 8:15 a.m. They were the "largest group of executions for crimes against a single victim in Virginia history."

After two years, six trials, five stays, ten judicial reviews and two denials of clemency, the Martinsville Seven came home for burial. Funerals began on Sunday, February 4 with others on Tuesday. There were no riots, no protests, and no lynchings. Martinsville remained quiet as it still does, both black and white. Interviewers tried over the years to talk to those involved including Charlie Martin, who would not discuss it.

As previously mentioned, Virginia started executing men in rape cases. Before the "Martinsville Seven," 45 black men lost their lives, plus the seven and three more after them with the last being in 1961 for a total of 55 black men to ZERO white men for the same crime. No white men were executed for raping a black woman during this same time. That is a compelling case for justice not being equal.

Judge Kennon C. Whittle went on to serve on the Virginia Supreme Court of Appeals from 1954 to 1961. He retired in 1965 after a return to the bench. He lived at Belleview on Chestnut Knob Road, which was built by Major John Redd of Revolutionary War fame. When Whittle died in 1967, his obituaries made no mention of the "Martinsville Seven." The silence was and is still deafening.

One writer stated that the trials for the "Martinsville Seven" were fair and they were no doubt guilty. They were victims of the laws of Virginia in their time, but it is still hard not to say they were the victims of legal murder. In 1976, the U. S. Supreme Court ruled in the case of Coker v. Georgia that capital punishment was unconstitutional in cases of rape.

Today, people in Martinsville, Virginia, do not like to talk about this case. The reader can learn more about the case in Eric W. Rise's *The Martinsville Seven: Race, Rape, and Capital Punishment*. He wrote, "At a time when African-Americans were beginning to assert their civil rights vigorously, the execution

provided a stark reminder of the harsh treatment reserved for

black who violated Southern racial codes."

Joe Henry Hampton

Booker T. Millner

Francis Grayson

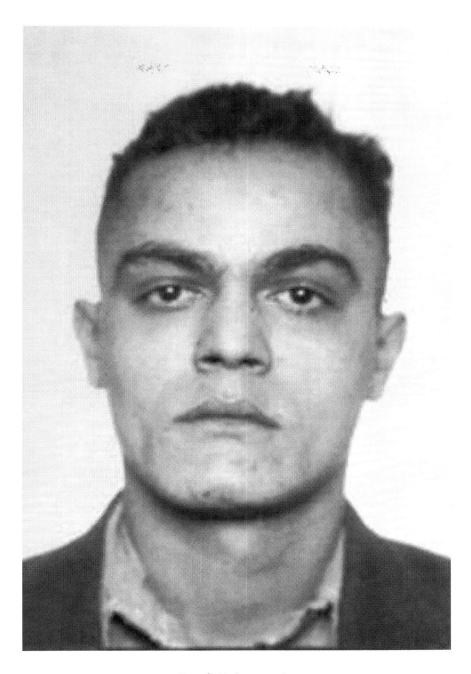

Frank Hairston, Jr.

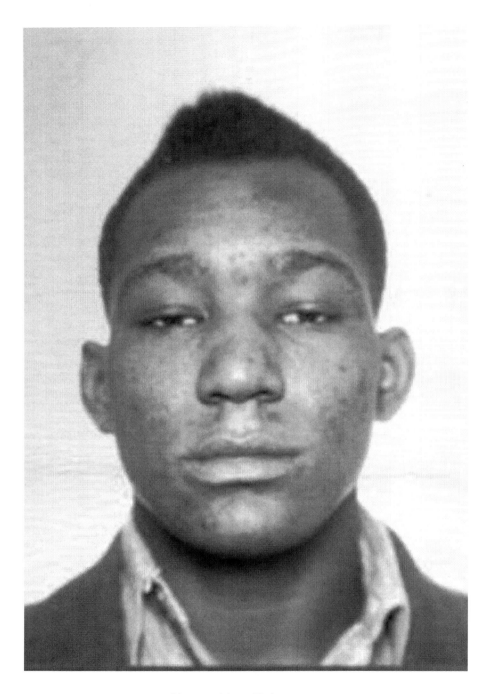

Howard Lee Hairston

James Lee Hairston

John Clabon Taylor

VOL. 60, NO. 207   N.E.A. Service   MARTINSVILLE, VIRGINIA.

The Virginia Supreme Court of Appeals today agreed to review the cases of seven Martinsville Negroes sentenced to death for rape. The seven are, left to right, Booker T. Millner, Frank Hairston, Jr., Howard Lee Hairston, Joe Henry Hampton, John Clabon Taylor, Francis DeSales Grayson, and James Luther Hairston.

Above, protests in support of the Martinsville Seven. Below, letter campaigns to save their lives.

Judge Kennon Whittle

Above, Athol, home of the Whittles in Martinsville, Virginia.
Below, efforts underway to save the Martinsville Seven.

Today, the site of the rape is along the Dick and Willie walking trail in Martinsville.

Virginia Governors: Above John S. Battle and below, William Tuck.

The Smith River Trail system includes the site of the rape.

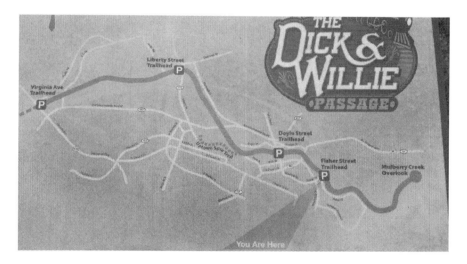

Hunter's Chapel Church has the graves of the murderer and victim of this chapter.

Chapter Six:

ARARAT'S LYNCH HOLLOW

In searching for information on life for African-Americans during the Civil War for my book on Patrick County's role that became *The Free State of Patrick: Patrick County Virginia in the Civil War*, I contacted Herman Melton of Pittsylvania County. He sent me a copy of his book *"Thirty-Nine Lashes—Well Laid On:" Crime and Punishment in Southside Virginia 1750-1950,* which contained the following information.

In September 1897, a twenty-two-year-old white man named Henry Walls lived in Ararat, Friend's Mission or The Hollow depending on what name the post office was using at that time. A member of the Cook family accused Walls of being in possession of a stolen saddle, and a confrontation ensued resulting in Walls threatening to run off the entire Cook family even if it meant burning down their home.

The following Friday, Walls tried to burn down the Cook home but was discovered by the only member of the family at home, Sadie. Tracks show that Sadie attempted to flee, but was pursued about seventy-five yards from the house and met her death due to a blow to the head, a throat slash, and several gashes to her body. Sadie survived this attack long enough to be discovered. Locals questioned her and although unable to talk revealed the identity of her assailant by squeezing Mrs. Epperson's hand when the latter mentioned Walls.

The next day Constable Tom Childress arrested Walls and imprisoned overnight until he could transport him to Stuart, Virginia, the county seat. Emotion running high in the area caused Sheriff Rufus Woolwine to venture to the area stopping for the night within a mile of the Childress home that night. A mob came, took Walls, and hung him in the hollow behind Hunter's Chapel Church just above the Ararat River between The Hollow Road and the Hunter's Chapel Road

Wall's tracks were identified as the assailant later, and there was evidence that he sexually assaulted Sadie Cook. The story made it into the *Lynchburg News* and the *New York Sun* reporting, "...there was practically no evidence to convict Walls of the crime. It is now believed that he was innocent. There is much indignation in the neighborhood against the mob."

If you want to find out about history in Ararat, want to double check your facts or if you want to have a cold drink and talk you would visit Carrie Sue Culler. Her mother, a Pedigo, descended from the family that lived next door to J. E. B. Stuart and her mind, still clear, as a bell is always willing to share much oral tradition until her death at age 107. She let me see a book by Charles Seaton entitled *After Conestoga Wagons and a Peruvian Odyssey* that held the following information.

Seaton writes that the leader of the vigilante mob was thirty-five-year-old Charles Walter Taylor, son of Surry County Sheriff Samuel Taylor. Charles married Sara Elizabeth Pedigo at the end of 1884 and thus the connection to Carrie Sue. Taylor placed the rope around the neck of Walls. Almost immediately, Taylor realizing the trouble, he was in left for California, eventually sent for his wife and children, and started a new life. Charles Taylor lived until 1942

As previously mentioned, a folktale rose from the murder and lynching, and it metamorphosed into a tale used to scare children into coming home before dark called "Raw-Headed-Bloody-Bones." The story first told me by Gray Guynn was that a monster lived in Lynch Hollow with a hoe handle for a tail and this monster got boys who played hooky from school to go fishing in the Ararat River and did not get home before dark. This monster made a sound like "Shiffity Shiffity Thumpity Thumpity." For all this monster's powers, he could not open a gate or climb over a picket fence, which saved the boy quaking under his bed after barely escaping clutches of the monster of Lynch Hollow. The folktale no doubt comes from the combination of the name of a local family, the Moores, who patriarch was Rodeham aka Raw Head and the hoe handle comes from the tradition that a hoe was used to kill Sadie Cook. The murder of Sadie Cook and lynching of Henry Wall(s) was one of those events I heard of from an early age. I remember mowing the grass of the cemetery at Hunter's Chapel Church that holds the remains of both buried the same day in unmarked graves.

The Bowman House at the intersection of the Ararat Highway and The Hollow Road. Below, the view from the house looking towards the Blue Ridge Mountains with Lynch Hollow in the foreground.

Looking towards the Blue Ridge Mountains with Lynch
Hollow in the foreground.

The graveyard holds the remains of victim and murderer.

Charlie Lawson killed his family in December 1929.

Chapter Seven:

<u>LAWSON'S BLOODY CHRISTMAS</u>

On October 29, 1929, the stock market crashed on Wall Street in New York City. Two months later, the life of Arthur Lawson came crashing down around him in one of the worst murder/suicides in the history of our region when his father killed himself and his entire family except for his oldest son.

Charlie Lawson lived on the Brook Cove Road in Germanton, North Carolina, with his wife, Fannie, age 37 and their children. Arthur, age 19, the oldest son, lived with his sister, Marie, age 17, the oldest daughter. The other children included Carrie, age 12, Maybelle, age 7, James, age 4, Raymond, age 2, and Mary Lou, age 4 ½ months. Another son, William, died of pneumonia at age 6.

Known as the Christmas Massacre or Bloody Christmas, this crime has been covered in two books by Trudy J. Smith. First in 1990 with *White Christmas, Bloody Christmas*. The second and more detailed book *The Meaning of Our Tears: The True Story of the Lawson Family Murders Christmas Day 1929* came out in 2006 in hardback. This case reminds the author that with all the mass shootings and murders today that sadly nothing is new in the history of this nation.

There is much speculation about why this murder/suicide occurred, but this author believes it comes down to one thing. Charlie Lawson was mentally ill, or he was overwhelmed by guilt or shame. It is possible that it is a little of both, but no man kills his entire family and himself without there being serious issues and serious secrets in a family. None of us know how another person feels or what they think, but here is what happened.

Charlie married Fannie on March 12, 1911. They moved to Germanton to live near Charlie's brothers, Marion, and Elijah. They bought 114 acres on Brook Cove Road on April 30, 1927, for $3,200.

That same year of 1927, Charlie Lawson was digging a basement of his pack house on his farm. He needed a drainage ditch to let water escape from the structure. While using a mattock, he struck a rock or something hard in the ground causing the tool to rebound and strike him in the head. He visited a local doctor in Germanton with blood vessels broken on his scalp and two black eyes. The doctor later expressed that he did not think the damage caused the change in Charlie that led to the crime.

Others noted, after the fact, a change in the behavior of the man at the center of the crime. There were strange behaviors such as walking away from people in mid-conversation, frequent fights, and violent threats towards others. He made comments such as "I wouldn't mind dying if I could only take my family with me." Charlie got in a fight at a tobacco warehouse with an African-American man after the man ran into Charlie's leg twice. The man cut Charlie several times and resulted in a two-week hospital stay. Later, people claimed that the man came back years later and killed the family. No doubt, race came into this theory, and it does not fit with the fact that Charlie killed himself.

All the evidence in this crime comes from one source, and all the comments are hearsay not admissible in a court of law. People want to sensationalize actions of people, but after the fact makes any serious student very suspicious especially if there is only one source in such a vicious crime involving the death of young children.

In May 1929, Charlie and his oldest son, Arthur, came to blows over the cultivation of their tobacco crop. Arthur pushed to the breaking point by his father and told him, "You ain't going to whip me no more." Arthur had grown to a bigger man than his father and his absence on Christmas Day was thought to be the reason Charlie acted as he did because he knew Arthur could stop him from finishing his desperate crime. Charlie was afraid of his oldest son from other reports.

The summer of 1929 saw many events that affected the mind of Charlie Lawson. His wife, Fannie, gave birth to a daughter, Mary Lou, on August 26. The stress of a pregnancy and concern added to the angst felt by the man. Another problem was the terrible headaches that Charlie suffered through, ever since his accident with the mattock. He said that the "misery in my head is so bad, I can't stand it." He was not sleeping, and his behavior got stranger as the summer turned to fall.

The harvest of corn, wheat, and tobacco that fall proceeded with neighbors helping each other. Charlie became obsessed with his guns. Constantly, cleaning his multiple weapons. There were reports of Charlie crying in the middle of the night or people finding him in the middle of a cornfield crying or praying.

Family members reported that Fannie told them Charlie had something important he wanted to tell her, but he never did tell his wife the secret. This led to much speculation about a possible sexual relationship between father and daughter, the seventeen-year-old Marie.

A few weeks before Christmas, Ella May Johnson told that Marie spent the night with her and confessed to being pregnant by her father. Fannie had noticed her missing her period, and her father threatened her saying, "would be some killing done."

The community knew Charlie was a good shot. Deputy Sheriff William Gomer Burrows of Stokes County arrived at 5:30 a.m. on Thanksgiving Day to hunt with Charlie. Burrows left thinking Charlie was an "all right kinda fellow." Sadly, a month later he would feel differently.

Charlie told Fannie he was planning a surprise for Christmas. Two weeks before the holiday, Charlie took the whole family on the hour ride to Winston-Salem in his Ford truck. Charlie, Fannie, James, Raymond, and the baby, Mary Lou, sat up front. The other children sat behind them in a modified truck on bench seats. Charlie bought the whole family a new set of clothes, and they wore the new clothes to a nearby photographer's store for the famous picture of the family. They changed clothes and rode home. The next time the family wore the clothes was at their funerals.

On December 20, snow began to fall on Germanton, North Carolina. It was one of the worst winters in memory, and six to eight inches would fall.

On December 23, Charlie rode his mule, Tom, to Walnut Cove on a bitterly freezing day. He went to the bank and two days later was found with $60 in his wallet, a large amount of money for him at the time. One could speculate he withdrew all the money he had from the bank. His strange behavior was noted by those who saw him that day. Specifically, he lost his temper with the mule on the slippery and steep streets.

Christmas Day came on Wednesday, December 25, that year. The Christmas gift for the family was the new clothes and the trip to Winston-Salem for the photograph, so there were no presents under the tree that day.

Arthur and his cousin, Sanders, went rabbit hunting that morning with the Lawson dogs, Sam, and Queen. Another cousin, Odell Ashby, joined the pair. They hunted for two hours before going to Odell's house to get some more ammunition around 10 a.m. They made their way to other homes and then back to the Lawson house. Charlie joined in with the boys throwing cans up in the air and shooting at them.

Inside the house, Marie cooked a cake with raisins on top. Many neighborhood children visited and played in the yard with the Lawson kids. Abe Heath came by as he was "sweet on Carrie."

Arthur and Sanders walked to Germanton to buy some more ammunition to continue their hunting and shooting. Charlie refused to let them borrow his personal stash as he was planning a different use for his ammo. Charlie left the house with his rifle and went to the barn and got his shotgun.

Abe Heath left, and Charlie began stalking his own family, hiding behind the tobacco barn about 500 yards from the house. He and his repeating rifle, 12-gauge double barrel shotgun, and his single shot 12-gauge shotgun.

Carrie and Maybelle left the Lawson home headed towards the Elijah house nearby. Charlie met them. He shot Carrie first with the rifle. She put up her hand to ward off the shot, but it went through. Maybelle was next to die as she was shot in the back, trying to run away. Many neighbors claimed to have heard conversations and shots, but that was after the crime was known. Most probably thought the shots were just hunters. It is hard to imagine someone hearing Carrie saying, "Papa don't shoot me" and not doing anything about it. Charlie dragged his daughters into the barn and placed stones under their heads, folded their arms across their chests, and closed their eyes.

Fannie came out to get some wood and saw her husband approaching. She turned to run and got a shotgun blast, which destroyed her heart. Her blood ran off the porch into the snow, making it a bloody Christmas. Abe Heath returned after hearing the shot and saw the scene. Down at the main road, the mailman heard screams and shooting. Like many others, he claimed he thought it was just hunters.

Marie ran to the front porch, seeing her father dragging her mother. She returned to the house to get the poker from the fireplace. Charlie reloaded his gun and fired point blank into his oldest daughter's back, slamming her into the fireplace mantle breaking her teeth and wrist. The blast was so powerful that you could see through her body.

A neighbor boy, Hassell, looked Charlie in the eye with a "wild look" as if telling him to run or die. He ran out the back door. James and Raymond tried to hide from their father under a bed and the kitchen stove, respectively. Charlie pulled Raymond out and beat his head with the butt of a gun leaving him half under the stove. Charlie chased James and killed him the same way. Charlie killed the baby, Mary Lou, with the butt of one of his shotguns.

As the house went silent, Charlie put a pillow under his dead wife's head. He went upstairs leaving bloody handprints along the wall to get Marie's pillow and repeated the same kindness he showed his wife, but he slipped and fell in her blood. As he continued the macabre ritual of cradling his dead children's head, he realized one of his shotguns was damaged and left it in the house.

He took the single barrel shotgun and his rifle and left the house. Abe Heath arrived home with news of the killings. Abe's brother, Rufus, got in his car, got Charlie Wade Hampton, and went to get Arthur and Sanders. Abe was not allowed to return to the Lawson house.

Elijah Lawson and his sons, Fred and Claude, were out hunting. They went to the Lawson house and found the front door blocked by Fannie's body. They thought Charlie might still be in the house. Elijah Lawson came into this home with the same news.

Arthur arrived home and collapsed on the front porch overwhelmed by emotion. A rocking chair was brought from the house and placed near a bonfire built by local men. Arthur sat in the chair rocking and sobbing uncontrollably. Charlie Lawson's brother stood around the house, guarding it until the law arrived.

Sheriff John Taylor and Dr. Chester Helsabeck arrived. They found five bodies in the front room. No one knew where Charlie Lawson was and going in the house was a concern especially the upstairs. Deputy Robert Walker and Dr. Robert Bynum, who knew Charlie searched the house finding no one alive.

Charlie was one hundred yards away in a pine thicket with the family dogs, Sam, and Queen. He walked in circles, lighting matches to stay warm. A single shot echoed out. Charlie shot himself in the chest. The dogs left him and returned to the house when they heard voices. Men followed the dogs back to Charlie's lifeless body.

Deputies brought Carrie and Maybelle from the barn to the house. Uncle Marion Lawson took Arthur back to his home. Four deputies brought Charlie back to his home. Eventually, the entire family was placed on sleds and taken down the hill to waiting vehicles from the funeral home in Madison, North Carolina.

After completed autopsies, Charlie's brain ended up at Johns Hopkins in Baltimore but later was lost. Doctors noticed nothing abnormal in his brain.

The adage "Murder Sells" became clear with this hideous crime. As early as the next day, people started coming to the Lawson house to view the scene of the crime. Gawkers and souvenir hunters started taking property including blood from the victims.

On Friday, December 27, funerals were held with thousands of people descending on Browder Cemetery in Walnut Cove, North Carolina. Arthur and his Uncle Marion Lawson fell to their knees overcome with emotion. Elder Brown, a Primitive Baptist Preacher, said, "Why this thing has occurred, I don't know...God alone knows why this terrible deed was done." The caskets were open for Arthur to have one last view of his family. It took three hours for everyone else to walk by the bodies. There were six white coffins and one gray for Charlie.

The next day, Saturday, December 28, Charlie Wade Hampton got a Christmas card from Marie. She was sweet on the neighbor boy.

Reality soon hit Arthur as to keep the family farm, he owed $500 for the next payment. His Uncle Marion Lawson took control. They opened the site as a tourist attraction charging 25 cents for anyone over 12. Children were free. The "exhibit" included the single and double barrel shotguns and a replacement rifle as one of the neighbors had the original. They roped the house for a limited number of visitors at a time. The tour entered through the front door, kitchen, attic, and exited through the back door. Marie's raisin cake was still on the kitchen table. They had to put a clear cake dish over the desert as people started taking raisins off the cake. The clock on the mantle stopped at 1:25 p.m. Famous visitors including John Dillinger came to view the site. It allowed Arthur to pay off the debt and got over $30,000.

Rumors started about the house being haunted including a tale about the cook stove glowing "red hot" at midnight and the cradle rocking by itself. They became so prominent that even Arthur returned one night to see if the stove glowed. It did not.

On January 28, 1930, the farm's livestock, perishables, and farm equipment sold at auction. There was a song released on Columbia Records "The Murder of the Lawson Family" recorded by Walter "Kid" Smith in 1930.

Arthur Lawson known as "Buck" to his friends and family would spend many hours staring with his blue eyes into the fire. A local girl's father forbade his daughter to see him. He played Rook and began to drink heavily. At 6' 4", he worked as a bouncer. He married Nina Bibey and had four children. He worked for Uncle Marion. On May 5, 1945, a truck accident threw him out of the vehicle before it landed on him. He was dead at age 31 and was put beside the other members of his family he lost over fifteen years earlier.

Nina moved her children to California trying to forget the tragedy that consumed her husband's family. In the 1980s, the

Lawson farm was torn down. Today, the site is overgrown and hard to find.

The graves of the Lawson family are in the Browder Cemetery, where their tombstone says, "Not, now, but in the coming years, it will be a better land: We will read the meaning of our tears, and then, sometime we'll understand." After the crime, a tobacco bill of sale was found with Charlie's handwriting stating, "Blame no one but I...Trouble will cease."

There is no doubt that the blame lies with Charlie Lawson. His children and especially his oldest son, Arthur, who had to live with the aftermath of the horrific event deserve our sympathy. No one can imagine the survivor guilt Arthur must have endured and questioned what he might have done to stop his father, but his father planned it, so he would not be there to stop him.

Charlie Lawson obsessed and planned the death of his family. Whether was due to a blow to the head or the incest with his oldest daughter, it shows in many ways how things have changed little in our nation. Regardless, of the laws on gun control, controlling mental illness is still the cause of many of these tragedies, and until we find a way to get control of it, we

will continue to have incidents such as these.

The Lawson family.

Back row left to right, Arthur, Marie, Charlie, Fanny, and baby
Mary Lin. Front row, James, Maybelle, Raymond, and Carrie.

Above, the Lawson cabin and the below, the barn on the Lawson farm, where the murders occurred.

Above, inside the Lawson cabin. Below, the funeral of the Lawson family.

The Browder Cemetery in Stokes County, North Carolina.

Bill Cochrane was the victim in the following chapter.

Chapter Eight:

<u>MOUNT AIRY'S FRANKLIN STREET BOMBER</u>

New Year's Eve, December 31, 1951, started as a quiet morning on Franklin Street in Mount Airy, North Carolina. My grandparent's Erie and Idell Bates Perry lived nearby in the area when not working at one of the myriad of textile sock mills in the town. Hometown boy Andy Griffith was teaching high school in Goldsboro, North Carolina. My father was at Lees-McCrae College in Banner Elk, North Carolina.

William Homer Cochrane, Jr., a 24-year-old agricultural teacher at nearby White Plains School lived at the corner of McCargo and Franklin Streets. He got into his pickup truck to head for his first day of class after the Christmas holiday, where he had taught for three years. William parked his 1951 pickup truck on Friday, and it sat there the entire weekend unmoved. It was a foggy morning with temperatures in the thirties. Cochrane turned the ignition key and pressed the starter button.

Cochrane lived with his wife of four months, the former Imogene Moses, in the Moody Apartments. She was the Assistant Surry County Home Demonstration Agent. She left about fifteen minutes before the explosion. The couple used her car over the weekend.

Suddenly, the calm broke with the sound of an explosion that threw Cochrane through the roof and twelve feet from his truck, but not killing him. He lost a leg, and the blast mangled him badly including an injured arm. The bomb blew out windows on the top floor of the apartment building where the Cochranes lived. Searchers found parts of the truck on the other side of the building after being blown over the top of the structure. The killer connected the blasting cap to the truck's electrical system.

Mrs. A. B. Council, Warna, the Society Editor of the *Mount Airy Times*, a now defunct newspaper, called the police at 8 a.m. saying "Come down here. There has been a horrible explosion. May be gas." *Mount Airy Times* newspaper editor W. M. Johnson arrived on the scene, but it was too foggy for "Mr. Will" Johnson to take pictures. He was filling in for his son, W. M. Johnson, Jr., who was on his honeymoon.

Policemen Howard Tolbert and Jack Ledford arrived about 8:25 a.m. It was a different time as the police allowed the media to take pictures of the scene. They found Cochrane's shoe in a pool of blood four feet from the truck, but they found his keys, leather notebook, and teaching assignment still laying on the seat of the truck. Chief Boone and Captain W. Howard Sumner arrived and roped off the crime scene.

William told those who came to his aid, "Somebody help me. I don't want to die" through the shock of his injuries. Cochrane was taken to the nearby Cherry Street Hospital in Mount Airy, where Dr. Moir Martin, formerly of Stuart, Virginia, and Dr. T. C. Britt worked for five hours on Cochrane amputating both his legs above the knees. Deputy Harry Monday visited him after surgery as no one was sure that he was not still in danger. Monday got Cochrane a "Coke," but the injured man was unable to drink it. William H. Cochrane, Jr. died at 9:45 p.m.

White Plains School dismissed on Tuesday and on Thursday over 3,000 people came to Moody's Funeral Home, which is today a block away from the corner of Franklin and McCargo, but was then on Market Street. The funeral was held in Franklin, North Carolina, where William H. Cochrane, Sr. was the Police Chief. His father told the Mount Airy Police Chief that his son "hadn't an enemy in the world."

North Carolina State Bureau of Investigation sent agent John Edwards from Elkin and Guy Scott of Winston-Salem to investigate. Mount Airy Police Chief Boone personally carried the bomb fragments to the Federal Bureau of Investigation. Another SBI agent Willis Jessup also became involved in the investigation. The Mount Airy Board of Commissioners offered a $2,500 reward for information about the killing. North Carolina Governor Kerr Scott offered another $400.

Men Imogene dated at Appalachian State Teacher's College and men she dated while teaching in Chatham County, North Carolina, were questioned. Investigators questioned people who bought dynamite such as Ed Draughn of W. E. Merritt

178

Hardware. Draughn claimed the four sticks of dynamite and five electric caps were to open his well. Many wells in the area were going dry causing more purchases of dynamite.

Mount Airy News Reporter R. J. Berrier often wrote of this incident over the years. I enjoyed his articles about local history and this Franklin Street bombing was one of those incidents. There were "no clues and no motive" for killing Cochrane. This story was about to get even stranger.

On April 7, 1954, Imogen Moses Cochrane, now living in Edenton, North Carolina, opened her car door and spotted what she could not believe a cardboard box. She kicked it and pulled it out from under the front seat. It was a booby trap bomb in her vehicle in a cardboard box about 6x10 inches. There was no cover, and she saw "tiny pebbles, copper wire, and a flashlight in the corner." She backed away from her vehicle and called her landlord George Hoskins. She drove the car the previous night and returned about 8 p.m., locked her doors after she arrived on Blount Street, but she parked on a side street.

Hoskins came out of the house and moved the box out of the car and took it across the road. He called Edenton Police Chief George Dial. Dial arrived, removed the "crude homemade device" and took it to his headquarters, where it exploded while he entered the building, burning him badly on his head and hands.

This second bomb consisted of picture frame wire with a flashlight battery with blasting powder and matches and was not near as complex or powerful as the Mount Airy bomb. Investigators thought the bomb was an attempt to scare Imogene into not marrying another man.

Imogene described as "a slender brunette" had recently resigned from her job as Chowan County Home Demonstration Agent. She was going to marry George Adam Byrum, a local businessman and councilman on April 24.

North Carolina State Bureau of Investigation agents John Edwards and Guy Scott arrived in Edenton with one common denominator, Imogene, from the earlier bombing. During the time between Christmas 1951 to Easter 1954, there had to be a connection between the two crimes separated by two years and three hundred miles.

For two years, the focus of the case aimed at George Henry Smith, a family friend of Imogene's. After the Edenton bombing, SBI agents Jessup and Assistant Director James Bradshaw traveled to Pittsboro, North Carolina, in Chatham County to confront Smith. They found him at the service station that employed him. Nervously, he agreed to allow the agents to vacuum out his car as other agents were vacuuming Imogene's car.

Smith left work, went home, and parked. Police watched Smith as Mount Airy Police Chief W. H. Sumner had also headed to Pittsboro with former chief Monte W. Boone. They too had one person in mind, William Cochrane, Jr.

Smith walked into a field and the woods. Agents lost contact with him, and he did not return. About 9 a.m. the next morning they found him leaning against a tree. George Henry Smith committed suicide on his father's wooded farm between

Pittsboro and Goldston the previous afternoon. Smith shot himself in the heart as law enforcement closed in on him.

Smith lived about a mile from Imogene growing up, and she rebuffed Smith's advances because she considered him just a friend, but Smith's "inner feelings ran much deeper and stronger." Investigators discovered Smith went to Mount Airy before Cochrane's death. Granules from both Imogene's and George Henry Smith's car matched leaving no doubt that he was the bomber.

Twice bombers killed a man who won the heart of the lady in question in Mount Airy. Nothing shows the difference between the town that Andy Griffith fictionally based his Mayberry on *The Andy Griffith Show* because the only dynamite that endangered anyone on the television show was a goat that liked to eat dynamite, a loaded goat.

The site of the bombing on Franklin Street in Mount Airy.

Bill and Imogene Cochrane were the victims of the bomb on
Franklin Street in Mount Airy.

Apartment building on Franklin Street where the bomb went off.

Grave of William Letcher in Ararat, Virginia.

Chapter Nine:

<u>REVOLUTIONARY MURDER IN THE HOLLOW</u>

In the summer of 1780, Lord Charles Cornwallis was coming through the Carolinas heading for a date with Nathaniel Greene at the Battle of Guilford Courthouse in March 1781 and a date with George Washington at Yorktown, where he surrendered and ended the American Revolution. The pro-British Loyalists or Tories became emboldened by the presence of a large British force close by and looked for targets on the Patriot side. Living on the banks of the Ararat River at his farm called Laurel Hill in present day Ararat, Virginia, was William Letcher, his wife Elizabeth Perkins Letcher, married in 1778, and their recently born daughter, Bethenia.

The story of the first people of European descent at Laurel Hill begins in Great Britain. Giles Letcher was born in Northern Ireland, but like so many people, he came to Virginia and settled near Petersburg. He married Hannah Hughes of Welsh descent and started a family. Letcher began a "successful mercantile business," but family tradition holds he lost it to fire. In 1741, he bought 135 acres north of the James River in Henrico County and began a slow migration up the river to the foothills of the Blue Ridge Mountains. By 1747, Giles Letcher owned land and the following year witnessed a deed transfer in Goochland County. In 1781, he bought 265 acres on Raccoon Creek, a tributary of the Rivanna River, in Fluvanna County.

The Letcher family connected to many important personages. Giles Letcher's first son, Stephen, was the father of Governor Robert Letcher of Kentucky. Robert Letcher served in the U. S. Congress as Minister to Mexico and on January 1, 1825, acted as a go between with Henry Clay and John Quincy Adams in the "corrupt bargain" that led to Adam's election as President in 1826. Robert Houston married Margaret Davidson and their son Samuel Houston, and his wife Elizabeth Paxton were the parents of General Sam Houston (1793-1863) of Texas. Sam Houston served as Congressman and Governor of Tennessee, then moved to Texas and became a leader of the independence from Mexico. He served as President of the Republic of Texas and then Senator and Governor from the State of Texas. In 1861, Houston opposed secession from the United States.

The third son of Giles Letcher, John, married Mary Houston, an aunt of Sam Houston, of Texas fame. John and Mary's son, William Houston Letcher, married Elizabeth Davidson and produced Virginia's first Civil War Governor John Letcher. Giles and Hannah Letcher had another son, James, and a daughter, Sarah.

William Letcher was born to Giles and Hannah Letcher around 1750, this author believes, in Goochland County. William, the second son, was described as a man of fine appearance and greatly beloved and esteemed.

On November 20, 1778, William Letcher married Elizabeth Perkins and moved to Henry County, present-day Patrick County. Elizabeth, born on May 13, 1759, to Nicholas and Bethenia Hardin Perkins, and grew up at Perkins Ferry in Halifax, now Pittsylvania County.

The first Nicholas Perkins came to Virginia in 1641 and settled in Charles City County. His son, also Nicholas married Sarah Childress, lived in Henrico County and produced a son Constantine.

He married Ann Pollard, lived in Goochland County. William and Elizabeth were both descended from Nicholas Perkins and Sarah Childress. Sarah Perkins married Thomas Hughes and their daughter Hannah married Giles Letcher.

Elizabeth's brother Peter Perkins married Agnes Wilson and built the historic home Berry Hill near Danville on land willed to him by his father. The name of the home comes from the large number of soldiers from both sides of the American Revolution believed buried on the property. Today, a large cemetery holds many prominent members of the family including J. E. B. Stuart's sister, Columbia, who married into the Hairston clan.

On August 2, 1856, John Letcher, future Governor of Virginia wrote of William Letcher, "He chose for his residence a spot in the southwest corner of Patrick County, Virginia, called The Hollow. It derives its name from the circular bend, which the mountains make around it. The Blue Ridge makes a semi-circular sweep halfway around it on the west and the Slate Mountain and Little Mountain on the east and south. The Ararat with its waters, as clear as crystal, and as swift as the arrow shot from the bow, traverse this whole valley from north to south and then empties into the Yadkin. On one of the gentle swelling hills, that lifts its head on the banks of this stream Mr. Letcher established his home."

On July 25, 1779, Letcher appeared on the payroll list of Captain David Carlin's Henry County Militia. In telling the story of William Letcher, each generation and biographer of General Stuart promotes him one grade in rank. He begins as Captain in J. E. B. Stuart's first biography and is a colonel by the last book in 1986. The highest rank found in official papers from Carlin's Militia lists him as a corporal.

Others listed include James and William Steward along with John and Edward Stewart. These other Stuart/Stewarts lived west of the Ararat River on a tributary appropriately named Stewart's Creek near the present day welcome centers along Interstate 77. In 1786, Surry County, North Carolina records showed Charles and Edward Stewart living close to their parents John and Susannah Fulkerson Stewart. John came from Delaware via Augusta County, Virginia, after certainly crossing from Scotland via Northern Ireland. Other Stewarts listed in Surry

County records are as follows. James, William, John, Hamilton Stewart living in Captain Hugh Armstrong's District. Nathaniel Stewart is listed as the head of household including Charles, Nathaniel, Jacob, James, and Joshua in 1786. Interestingly, Daniel Carlin lived on the waters of Stewart's Creek.

In August 1779, Henry County recommended William Letcher to the Governor of Virginia as a Commissioner of the Peace along with other prominent persons including Abram Penn, Patrick Henry, Archaelous Hughes and John Marr. On November 25, Letcher took the oath of office as Justice of the Peace and attended a counterfeiting trial.

No evidence exists that the Letchers owned land along both sides of the Ararat River. In April 1749, John Dawson, Joseph Cloud, and James Terry received a land grant of 12,000 acres from Virginia. In June 1753, David Bell took possession of 2,816 acres that included present-day Laurel Hill.

It is through the Perkins family that William and Elizabeth Letcher came to present day Patrick County. John Marr married Susannah Perkins, sister of Elizabeth Perkins Letcher. Constantine

Perkins married John's sister Agatha Marr. Marr's sons had a business relationship with the Perkins Family. John Marr died in Henry County before 1797. Marr, a land speculator, bought the land that is the Laurel Hill Farm in 1790 from John Dawson. Two years later, he owned over 3,000 acres in the county.

The Perkins family connection stayed strong in the area. In 1801, Thomas Perkins bought a plantation in adjoining Surry County and named it Mount Airy. In 1819, Thomas' son Constantine inherited Mount Airy along with land on present-day Main Street, where he built the first of many lodging establishments (most named Blue Ridge). The Perkins home, Mount Airy, was located on high ground above the Ararat River between Hamburg Street and Quaker Road in Mount Airy, North Carolina. In 1780, Thomas Smith purchased 400 acres nearby for fifty shillings. The property contained a large granite outcropping. Today it is the largest open-faced granite quarry in the world operated by North Carolina Granite Corporation in Mount Airy, North Carolina.

Elizabeth and William Letcher left little documentation except for a list of possessions and the major events in their lives. They grew corn and tobacco in the bottomland along the river. They held livestock including twenty head of cattle, ten hogs, and five horses. There were nine slaves named David, Ben, Witt, Abraham, Dick, Look, Nunn, Randolph, and Craft. William Letcher's estate inventory located in the Henry County courthouse includes many of the household and farm items that you would expect. Among these items were saddlebags, rifles, three feather beds, and a looking glass.

On March 21, 1780, Elizabeth gave birth to her first child, Bethenia. This small child became the connection that led to a famous grandson's birth at Laurel Hill over fifty years later. Bethenia's daughter wrote of William Letcher at this time that, "He had the promise of long years of happiness and usefulness and domestic felicity, but a serpent lurked in his path, for whom he felt too great a contempt to take any precautions." The clouds of war reached the home of William and Elizabeth Letcher that summer with tragic results in the form of Tories, those loyal to the

British. John Adams said of the Tories, "A Tory here is the most despicable animal in the creation. Spiders, toads, snakes are their only proper emblems."

The same day Bethenia was born, Virginia Governor Thomas Jefferson wrote to Colonel William Preston in Montgomery County stating, "I am sorry to hear that there are persons in your quarters so far discontented with the present government as to combine with its enemies to destroy it." It was four years since this famous Virginian had penned the words of The Declaration of Independence.

On March 29, the British began a siege of Charleston, South Carolina, resulting in the surrender of the city on May 12, 1780. This marked a change in British strategy to a southern front. Up to this time, the opposing armies fought most of the battles in the corridor between Philadelphia and Boston.

It was the time of Banastre Tarleton for the British and Francis Marion "The Swamp Fox" for the Whigs or Patriots. On May 29, Tarleton defeated and then massacred the Patriots under Colonel Abraham Buford at the Waxhaws in South Carolina.

Tarleton refused to accept the surrender of the men and killed or wounded nearly 300. Four days later General Henry Clinton, the British commander in America issued a proclamation telling, "Anyone not actively in support of the Royal government belonged to the enemy and was outside the protection of British law."

With the presence of a large army in the region, the Tories began an aggressive campaign against Patriot groups. Historians estimate the population evenly divided over the cause of independence with one-third in favor, one-third indifferent and one-third pro-British. Political, religious, and even personal feelings directed the decisions of those involved and made for a volatile situation.

Lord Charles Cornwallis commander of the British commented on it this way, "In a civil war there is no admitting of neutral characters and those who are not clearly with us must be so far considered against us, as to be disarmed, and every measure taken to prevent their being able to do mischief." Cornwallis' opponent in the Southern Campaign, Nathaniel

Greene, said, "The whole country is in danger of being laid waste by the Whigs and Tories who pursue each other with as much relentless fury as beasts of prey." One participant summed up this civil war within the American Revolution in the following statement, "The virtue of humanity was totally forgot."

Documentation about Tory activity in the region exists. The Moravian settlers in nearby Forsyth County, North Carolina, often spoke of them in their diaries. Today, Tory Creek in nearby Laurel Fork on the Blue Ridge holds to be a traditional hiding place for those loyal to the Crown. One revolutionary war soldier, James Boyd, who served in Captain James Gidens militia from Surry County, North Carolina, stated in his pension application details about the hangings of Joseph Burks, Mark Adkins, Adam Short, William Kroll (Koil) and James Roberts for being Tories.

Tradition holds that William Letcher was a leader among the local people in support of the patriot cause and separation from Great Britain. Letcher left no doubt about his feelings, and this made him a target. As a member of the local militia, he may have been involved in several small battles against the pro-British sympathizers in the region. There is no evidence that Letcher took part in any major campaigns with the Continental Army or was ever a member of a mainline military unit. His granddaughter wrote of him, "He was very active in hunting them from their hiding places. He would frequently go alone, armed only with a shotgun, into the most inaccessible recesses of the mountains, exploring every hiding place...he knew it was for the Tories, who concealed themselves in the daytime but came forth in darkness and secrecy... William Letcher had proclaimed that he would lay down his life before one of them should lay a finger on his property. Hall used this remark to incite the Tories against him; reporting also his known enmity and activity in hunting them down, and representing their property as unsafe so long as William Letcher lived."

William Hall lived in Surry County, North Carolina, south of Letcher along the Ararat River. John Letcher mentions Hall's home, a meeting place for Tories, in the 1856 letter about Letcher.

Letcher's granddaughter continued her narrative about her grandfather. "Late one night, the Tories disguised as 'fiends' burned Letcher's smokehouse full of meat. Awakened by the fire and smell, Letcher scattered them with gunfire. One of the Tories reportedly replied from the darkness, 'I am Hell-Fire Dick. You will see me again.' Letcher oblivious to the danger continued a normal life as a farmer with his wife, newborn daughter, and slaves."

Oral tradition abounds today in Patrick County about the death of William Letcher. One version has Letcher shot from a nearby ridge while stepping out onto his porch. Another has him shot through a window of his home by a coward lurking outside at night.

The most romantic and accepted story tells that Letcher was in his fields on August 2, 1780, when a stranger came to the house and asked Elizabeth Letcher about her husband's whereabouts. She replied that he would be back shortly and invited the visitor to stay. When Letcher entered, the man named himself as Nichols, a local Tory leader, and said, "I demand you in the name of His Majesty." Letcher replied, "What do you mean?"

Nichols shot Letcher. The Tory fled the home leaving the dying Patriot in the arms of his wife, his last words being, "Hall is responsible for this." William Hall fled towards Kentucky, but Indians along the Holston River killed his entire family.

William Nichols born in Granville County, present-day Orange County, North Carolina, about 1750, married Sarah Riddle in 1770 the daughter of Colonel James Riddle, a prominent Surry County Tory. In 1771, a tax list of Surry County listed Nichols, who served in the local militia for the Patriots, but received harsh treatment for "bad conduct" and swore to seek revenge after he was discharged. Letcher was his first victim.

Reaction to Letcher's death was immediate. On August 6, Colonel Walter Crockett in Wythe County believing the murderers were "Meeks and Nicholas...assembled 250 men at Fort Chiswell and was about to march against the Tories on the New River. He reported that one Letcher had been murdered...it is generally believed a large body of those wretches are collected in The Hollow." The death of Letcher so stirred up the area that they hung the Tories "like dogs" including a group hanging in nearby

Mount Airy, North Carolina. When the wives of the doomed men "cried and lamented the fate of their husbands," they were "well whipped for sorrowing for a set of rogues and murderers."

Colonel William Preston in Montgomery County wrote Governor Jefferson on August 8 stating, "A most horrid Conspiracy amongst the Tories in this Country being providently discovered about ten Days ago obliged me Not only to raise the militia of the County but to call for so large a Number from the Counties of Washington and Botetourt that there are upwards of four hundred men now on Duty exclusive of a Party which I hear Colonel Lynch marched from Bedford."

Another pensioner, William Carter, speaks of "a great excitement was produced by the murder of a distinguished Whig, William Letcher, who was shot down in his own house by a Tory in the upper end of Henry County. Captain Eliphaz Shelton commanded a company of militia in which Carter was sergeant. Ordered by his captain to summon a portion of the company to go in pursuit of the murderer, he rode all night, collected twenty or thirty men early the next morning and pushed for the scene of the murder. The murderer and the Tories with whom he was connected had fled to the mountains where the detachments pursued them but failed in overtaking them and returned home after an absence of a week or more. He had scarcely returned home when the Tories returned to the same neighborhood and committed a good many robberies."

James Boyd's pension application states that Nichols and others murdered Letcher. Militia companies including those of Shelton, Lyon, and Carlin of Virginia and Gidens of North Carolina combined to make a force of over 200 men. He continues that Captain Gidens captured Nichols within two weeks, but mentions that it was at Eutaw Springs, a battle that occurred on September 8, 1781, in South Carolina.

Another account tells of "nine prisoners were captured, and on our return, two Nichols and Riddle out of the nine were hung...Tories Nichols and Riddle were hung in consequence of it appearing that they had been concerned with robbing a house." This account mentions that they were involved in robbing a house of "one Letcher murdered by Meeks and Nichols." Whenever

Patriots captured William Nichols tradition holds they hung him in chains and left him unburied. His motive for killing Letcher was in a letter found on his person after execution from the British offering a reward for every Patriot he killed.

On August 16, 1780, Cornwallis defeated Patriot General Horatio Gates at the Battle of Camden, South Carolina, and by the end of September, the British moved into that "nest of hornets" known today as Charlotte, North Carolina.

The cause Letcher gave his life for rebounded with Patriot victories at King's Mountain on October 7 and a week later at the Shallow Ford of the Yadkin River. In 1781, Virginian Daniel Morgan crushed Banastre Tarleton at the Battle of Cowpens on January 17. Nathaniel Greene lost to Cornwallis at the Battle of Guilford Court House on March 15 where Major Alexander Stuart fought. The road to Yorktown opened, and the surrender of Cornwallis to George Washington came on October 19, 1781, resulting in a victory for the United States of America, a little more than a year later with the signing of a peace treaty on November 30, 1782.

Today, William Letcher rests in the bottomlands along the Ararat River in Patrick County's oldest marked grave. His tombstone placed by his daughter before her death in 1845 states the following. "In memory of William Letcher, who was assassinated in his own house in the bosom of his family by a Tory of the Revolution, on the 2nd day of August 1780, age about 30 years. May the tear of sympathy fall upon the couch of the brave." The white marble stone from a Richmond stonecutter, William Mountjoy, from the corner of Main and Eight Streets.

Over the years, this author often imagined a young man standing in front of the grave with eyes down reading the inscription and then slowly raising his head to view the bottomland along the river. The land full of the life of growing crops with the mountains shaded by the blue mist filled him with pride. He had grown from this very soil, and it was here that he always called home. The young army officer's uniform was blue, and the summer sun reflected off the polished buttons. He placed his hat with the large dark plume on his head, saluted and turned to mount his horse. He galloped off to splash through the river and up the hill to the site of his birth, his waiting family, and his destiny. It was the summer of 1859, and First Lieutenant James Ewell Brown Stuart of the First United States Cavalry was home for the last time. As I write this, the grave is the only piece of the history from the Stuart Family that the young man would recognize if he came back today.

We should not lose sight of the irony of William Letcher's great-grandson losing his life eighty-four years later at nearly the same age fighting for what he believed was a second American Revolution. While it might be a stretch to say that Letcher's life and example led J. E. B. Stuart to a life in the military, it would not be hard to imagine a young man's fascination with brave ancestor fighting and dying for something he believed. This strong influence inculcated a strong love of home and a heroic legend he felt he must live up to.

The grave of William Letcher at the J. E. B. Stuart Birthplace in Ararat, Virginia.

The Grave of William Letcher is the oldest in Patrick County with an inscription. It reads.

" In memory of William Letcher, who was assassinated in his own house in the bosom of his family by a Tory of the Revolution, on the 2nd day of August, 1780, age about 30 years. May the tear of sympathy fall upon the couch of the brave."

This memorial is believed to have been placed by Letcher's daughter, Bethenia, before her death in 1845.

It was carved by William Mountjoy, a stonecutter from the corner of 8th and Main Street, Richmond, Virginia.

This structure & improvements was made possible by a generous donation from Jonathan Old of Greenwich, Connecticut, a direct descendant of William Letcher.

THE FAYERDALE
TRAGEDY
FAIRY STONE
STATE PARK

BY ELMER R. HAYNES

Chapter Ten:

TRAGEDY AT FAYERDALE

The waters of Fairy Stone State Park are calm and placid on most summer days, but in the past, before the lake backed up onto Goblintown Creek, there was a town there called Fayerdale. The town was a hub for the iron forge business that began many believe as far back as the 1700s. The White Hairston family pronounced HAR-ston not Hair-ston as the African-Americans, who were once their slaves say it, for many generations controlled the budding industry.

Jack Williamson writes on his wonderful website about the History of Fayerdale that George Hairston died leaving over http://www.angelfire.com/folk/goblintown_mill 20,000 acres of land in Patrick and Henry Counties that included the site of Fairy Stone State Park in 1827. In 1836, the Union Iron Works Company began. Slave labor mined the iron ore, and eventually, railroads hauled it out to nearby places such as Roanoke, Virginia.

There is even a story, apocryphal, that iron from the forges went into the *CSS Virginia* better known as Merrimac as it was once a United States ship. The *CSS Virginia* fought the *USS Monitor* in the first battle of ironclads in the War Between the States in Hampton Roads in 1862.

The iron mines ran from 1780 until 1911. By 1900, there were 400 mine workers, 1,000 lumber, and railroad employees, included in a population of 2,000 in the town that no longer exists. The last five years furnaces smelted the iron ore and shipped it as pig iron.

Fayerdale came from Mr. and Mrs. Frank Hill. F for Frank. Ayer from the misses' middle name and dale was a Mr. Lafferty's middle name, thus F-Ayer-Dale. Henry and Ruth Hall owned a hotel, and their sons ran a narrow gauge railroad that ran to Philpott, Virginia. You can still see signs of the train when they drain the lake at Fairy Stone from time to time for maintenance. Tom Elgin ran the railroad depot, general store, and the post office.

In a book about true crime and murder, it is understood that when you have men, moonshine, and guns, there is going to be murder. This chapter comes from one source a book titled *The*

Fayerdale Tragedy by Elmer R. Haynes. Any good historian is always leery of using only one source when writing, but this story has become such a tale in our area that it would be a crime not to include it in this book. Haynes was a second cousin to Euel, Maynard, Dave Cox, and "Jack" Hall was a great uncle of the author. All four of these men lost their lives in the pages to follow.

One can imagine that in a "mining town," there were drunken fights and that led to violence. Haynes writes that eleven murders happened at the site near the beach at Fairy Stone State Park. The people are only memories, and the town of Fayerdale is under the water, forgotten except by the few of us who like local history in Patrick and Henry Counties in Virginia.

Euel Cox described as a farmer, merchant, and bootlegger lived in a two-story house a little over two miles from the beach at the park that included two maids. He ran a general store located near the state park visitor center today that sold groceries, clothing, toys, hardware, and guns. Married to Mae Turner, Euel took care of things "outside" the store, while Mae managed inside the store.

The trouble began on Sunday, September 3, 1922, when an African-American Harvey Smith entered Cox's store. Smith used "abusive language" on one of Cox's employees. When Cox intervened, Smith tried to strike Cox, who in turn shot Smith, but not seriously wounding him as he was treated and released in Martinsville.

Cox ran a garage that employed two mechanics. He had a car collection himself that included eight cars, two Cadillacs, Moon and Star, two Buicks, Chrysler, and a Dodge. In fact, Cox owned the first automobile, a Cadillac, in the area. Cox employed an African-American man called Pharaoh, who acted as chauffeur, even wearing a uniform. Cox employed drivers who delivered his liquor to places in North Carolina such as Reidsville and Greensboro. They drove as far away to exotic places such as West Virginia. While the roads at that time were "rough," Cox had cars on the road constantly.

Standing six-foot-tall, Euel Cox was always clean shaven and usually wore tailor-made suits. Haynes writes that he got three to four new suits every three months or so. Business was good and allowed Euel to have such a lavish lifestyle. Described as a "sharp dresser," Cox did not smoke or drink, ironically, and had a photographic memory, which no doubt came in handy for his multiple businesses. He visited Draper's Barbershop in Martinsville where he got a haircut, shave, massage and got his shoes shined, where he gave a $5 tip.

Haynes writes in his book that Euel Cox "helped more people in need than any other person in Patrick County." It was a different time then with little government intrusion even though Prohibition began in 1920 at the end of Woodrow Wilson's second term as President of the United States and lasted until 1933 in the first term of Franklin Roosevelt.

Cox was one of many in Patrick County responsible for the upkeep of roads that passed along his property. The Patrick County Order Books are full of references to people, who had this community service after the Civil War up through the early twentieth century.

Haynes writes that Cox owned land in Martinsville and Henry County including three lots in the city and two lots in

Koehler near Fieldale. Cox stored his alcohol at these locations and others. Also, he owned the "Old Dillion Place," in Henry County near Fayerdale, which he was renovating.

On September 4, 1922, Euel Cox and an employee, Arthur Vaughan spent the night at "Old Dillon Place." Work was to begin on the next day, a Tuesday. That morning the two went for breakfast at J. A. Adam's house, with Vaughan driving a Cadillac.

After eating Cox walked alone down to the bottomland he owned to see if it was ready for plowing. Three African-Americans, General Lee Scott, Harvey Smith, and the latter's brother Willie Smith approached Cox in a car. They opened fire on Cox with a .32 caliber Smith and Wesson revolver. Two shots hit Cox in the intestine that punctured him 17 times and a third shot striking his leg. Cox, not deterred, returned fire with his .38 caliber Smith and Wesson wounding Willie Smith as the brothers jumped out and ran towards Harvey Smith's home. General Lee Smith sat behind the wheel of the car dead as Euel Cox was true to his aim. When law enforcement arrived, the engine of the vehicle was still running.

In an amazing feat, Euel Cox walked to the top of the hill and got Ellis Dodson to drive him to the Lucy Lester Hospital in downtown Martinsville. Dodson returned to inform Mrs. Euel Cox of the incident. She drove herself and a daughter to the hospital. She hired two nurses to be with Euel constantly. Dr. Shackelford told Euel to prepare himself and get his affairs in order and operated on him.

Euel sensing his end was near apologized to his daughter, Minnie, age eight, for not being able to take her with him and to his wife for not spending more time with her and less time with his businesses. Euel Cox died at 11:30 a.m. on September 6, 1922, twenty-seven hours after being shot.

Harvey Smith went to jail in Stuart, while his brother, Willie, escaped to Ohio. Harvey got thirty years in prison and served twenty. He denied that he killed Euel Cox until his death in 1975. Willie remained free for 53 years after the shooting. Forever connected with this tragedy at Fayerdale, Ellis Dodson married Minnie Cox eight years later. He was 26, and she was 16.

After Euel Cox's death, Mae Turner Cox rented a house to Turner G. "Jack" Hall, a second cousin of Euel. Hall was married to a sister of Ernest Shelton connecting the Hall, Cox, and Shelton families and no doubt the business of violating the Prohibition laws of the United States. Sadly, tragedy was not through with these families including "Jack" Hall, Ernest Shelton, and the brothers Maynard and Dave Cox.

On February 5, 1927, "Jack" Hall swore out a warrant on Dave Cox in Stuart, Virginia, the county seat of Patrick County. A deputy was supposed to serve the warrant, but Haynes writes that Patrick County Sheriff Frank Mays "did not want to get involved since he was receiving payoffs by both the Cox brothers and Jack Hall." Hall and his companions were not deputized. Hall visited his mother's home on 10th Street in Fieldale, where she begged him not to try and arrest Dave Cox.

The next day, Ewell Nichols, a teenage boy, visited "Jack" Hall's still in present-day Fairy Stone State Park and offered some information for a pint of liquor. Nichols told Hall that the Cox brothers, Maynard, and Dave, reported the still, which was later destroyed by revenue officers, who claimed the Cox brothers did not report it, but you cannot get the genie back into the bottle once they are out.

Haynes writes that Hall and Binlow Shelton retaliated by raiding and destroyed a Cox brother's still and a large amount of liquor. Dave Cox searched for "Jack" Hall's second still, which was the property of Tom Shelton, the father of Ernest. Cox found the still and cut it up.

Hall went to get Ernest Shelton, who lived five miles north of Fayerdale and stopped at the latter's father's home. Tom Shelton told them, "Boys, you had better think it over before going down there to arrest one of the Cox's boys." Hall and Shelton continued to the former's home, where they bolstered their courage with a few drinks.

Big John Chaney's house in Fayerdale was the site of a community get together on Sunday, February 6, 1927, with over thirty children playing in the yard. Among the grownups were Maynard and Dave Cox. Maynard left after a couple of hours, but

Dave stayed complaining of not feeling well. Chaney offered him a place to lay down and rest or sleep it off.

Chaney saw "Jack" Hall and Ernest Shelton coming in the former's 1927 Ford Touring Car. The two went into the house looking for Dave Cox to serve the warrant.

Ewell Nichols ran down the hill to where the boat dock is today at the state park, where he met Maynard Cox and told him about Hall and Shelton. Maynard was driving a 1927 Chevy Roadster with the top laid back with his sisters, Clara, and Josie, along with Arthur Wickham. The group was on the way to nearby Fieldale to drop off Clara and then to Eden, North Carolina to drop off the Wickhams. Maynard Cox was eventually headed to Draper, North Carolina, where he was to work the next day.

Maynard ran up the hill with his sisters, while Wickham, who was "crippled" stayed in the car. Maynard entered the house from a side door to find his brother, Dave, with his hands up in the air with Hall and Shelton holding guns. Josie said, "Don't hurt Dave."

The story goes that Shelton got Dave's .38 Smith and Wesson, while the latter was still asleep and gave it to a "bystander." Hall told Dave to get up. Dave replied, "I will go anywhere you want me to go."

The homeowner Chaney said that when Maynard Cox walked into the house that Hall shot Dave twice with a .45 caliber Colt Army Automatic pistol. The shots went through the body and landed on the bed killing Dave instantly. Maynard responded by shooting and killed Hall with his .32 Colt. Ernest Shelton then shot and killed Maynard with his .38 pearl-handled Smith and Wesson. In a scene from a movie, Maynard Cox and "Jack" Hall fell at the same time.

Stray shots hit Miss Bettie Chaney, an aunt of the homeowner, taking off her thumb. While another shot hit Willie Cox, a cousin of Maynard and Dave Cox, in his front pocket, breaking his knife handle.

Big John Chaney got down and crawled into another room hoping to save his life, but he returned and was shot in the eye and through his earlobe, which did not injure him mortally, but he did catch a bullet in the leg. He played dead as he thought Shelton would want no witnesses.

Ernest Shelton walked outside and stated, "Someone hand me a gun. I've shot mine empty." He got .38 Smith and Wesson, a very popular brand at the time, which he believed was Dave Cox's weapon surrendered when they first entered the house. I find it interesting that the make and model of each gun fascinated Haynes in his little book as much as the people involved.

Shelton walked to Zack's Hancock's home, where Hall's car was left. He did not say a word. One bystander said he looked "blue as if he had a stroke."

John Abe Turner went into the Chaney house, finding Maynard and Dave Cox dead. "Jack" Hall was groaning "Oh Lordy" and soon died. Daniel Lewis Cox, father of the dead brothers, came and spent the night in a chair in the Chaney house. An Inquest was held the next day at 8 a.m. with Sheriff Frank Mays and a local doctor.

Tom Shelton paid local politician and attorney Murray Hooker, father of Judge John Hooker of our time, $1,900 to defend his son, Ernest. Hooker got Shelton acquitted.

The death over liquor was not over. Five years later, Ernest Shelton lost his life when he was "suddenly and ruthlessly murdered" five years, nine months and nine days later on November 15, 1932. Prohibition ended the next year.

It was a custom of the people of Appalachia to set up with dead bodies. Shelton was sitting with "Dump" Adkins, who was murdered by his own grandfather. "Dump" was just out of prison after serving thirteen years for murder himself.

Adkins' corpse was at the home of Ike Prater. Henry and his son, Robert, Holley arrived around midnight. They spied Shelton near a window and shot him six times in the stomach with a pistol. They entered the house, Henry with a double barrel shotgun and Robert with a single barrel shotgun. Henry hit Ike Prater over the head cracking his skull. Robert Holley left while Henry threatened Harold Quinn, who was present. Quinn picked up Ernest Shelton's .38 caliber Smith and Wesson and shot Henry Holley five times. There were now three dead bodies in the room.

While all this murder occurred, the iron ore business had continued. In 1905, multiple owners formed the Virginia Ore and Lumber Company. In 1925, T. W. Fugate paid $50,000 for the railroad and mining equipment. Junius B. Fishburn bought out his partners at the Virginia Ore and Lumber Company in 1933. He donated 4,868 acres to the Commonwealth of Virginia to become Fairy Stone State Park. The Civilian Conservation Corps began work on the park and by 1936 Fayerdale was "razed," and Goblintown Creek dammed.

So, ends the violence of the "Fayerdale Tragedy" and the beginning of the end of the town of that same name. Iron ore became unprofitable to mine and with the end of Prohibition so did bootlegging, or did it? During the Great Depression, World War Two, and the following decades people continued to make moonshine. Many did so as a way of surviving the harsh economic times.

Placid water now covers the town that was the site of industry and mayhem. People gather on the banks of the lake to search for the staurolite crystals shaped like crosses the story goes were the tears of fairies when told of the death of Jesus Christ. It is proper that someone associated with forgiveness has the final word on these matters.

Today the site of the Fayerdale shootings are part of Fairy Stone State Park along the Patrick/Henry/Franklin County borders.

Fayerdale Hall is the site of the house, where the shootings occurred.

Euel Cox

Euel and Mae Turner Cox

Ellis and Minnie Cox Dodson

Turner G. "Jack" Hall

Ernest Shelton

The railroad between Fayerdale and Philpott

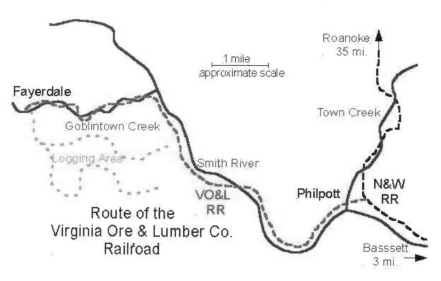

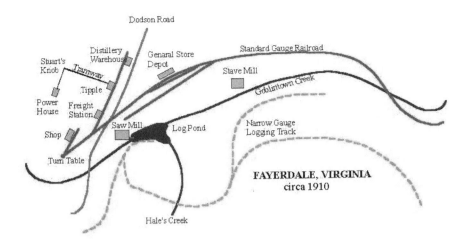

Dodson Road

Distillery
Warehouse
Stuart's
Knob
Tramway
Tipple
Power
House
Freight
Station
Shop
Turn Table
Saw Mill
Log Pond
General Store
Depot
Stave Mill
Coolntown Creek
Narrow Gauge
Logging Track
Standard Gauge Railroad

FAYERDALE, VIRGINIA
circa 1910

Hale's Creek

Fayerdale lies under the waters of Fairy Stone State Park

Making moonshine near Fayerdale. Below, look from the site of the Chaney House.

Kibler Valley in western Patrick County, Virginia.

Chapter Eleven:

<u>MURDER IN KIBLER VALLEY</u>

We live in an insulated world and do not notice the evil that is all around us. This is a story that hits close to home as I was about the same age as the victim and our mothers were the same age. We all lived in and around the place this crime occurred.

Every spring when I was a teenager in the late 1970s, my friends and I would spend the weekend that fishing season opened on the Dan River. While we really did not fish, but we did have an enjoyable time. Kibler Valley had a basketball court made for the children of the employees of the City of Danville, who ran the powerhouse that supplied electricity to the southside locale some seventy-five miles away. The Ararat and Claudville boys played there on sweltering summer days because it was so much cooler in the valley. Our only problem was when the ball managed to get knocked into the Dan River, and a mad dash occurred to retrieve it before play could resume.

Kibler Valley was a place of firsts for me. I think the first beer I ever drank was in Kibler Valley. The first time I ever woke up in the backseat of my 1964 snow white Volkswagen Beetle was in Kibler Valley. The first time that I might have encountered murder in my own life was in Kibler Valley. This is a case that hits close to home on many levels.

The Dan River falls out of the Blue Ridge Mountains by the Pinnacles of Dan through multiple dams and through the powerhouse at the top of Kibler Valley. It is an isolated part of the world that loses sunlight long before the surrounding area because the mountains on either side block the rays before and after they drop behind the peaks of the Appalachians.

Described as "the most dangerous man in Surry County, North Carolina, Virginia convicted Dennis Stockton of murder in March 1983." A former North Carolina SBI investigator speculated once to me that "Dennis might not have killed the Arnder boy, but I am sure he did something to deserve the death penalty." One of his own lawyers said of him, "If anyone ever looked like a killer, this was the guy."

There are still many questions about the crime including where it happened and who pulled the trigger that sent Kenneth

Arnder off this mortal coil. Some of these questions came into being because before Virginia executed Stockton. He denied vehemently that he committed the crime and, in a book, *Dead Run: The Shocking Story of Dennis Stockton and Life on Death Row in America* by Joe Jackson and William F. Banks, Jr.

Dennis Stockton was born on October 26, 1940, in Shelby, North Carolina, the second of four children. His childhood in southern North Carolina was a bucolic one, where he read Louis Lamour and dreamed of being a cowboy. The book about him claimed he had an IQ of 160 and was good enough to play professional baseball. Behind his "deep set blue eyes," laid the soul of a career criminal. His family moved to White Plains, just south of Mount Airy, North Carolina, when Stockton was twelve. The place is famous for the last home and burial place of Eng and Chang Bunker, the Siamese Twins, who traveled the world as performers.

Stockton's career as a criminal began when local law enforcement drug him from his tenth-grade classroom at Mount Airy High School for passing bad checks by forging his own father's name on the checks. For this, he got three to five years beginning a life that was spent mostly behind bars from ages 16 until 42. He was back in Mount Airy by 1960. Stockton blamed his problems on his abusive father, a World War II veteran, described as violent, who involved in illegal tobacco smuggling and bootlegging. Stockton implied that he was tagged early with being a homosexual after getting advances from prominent men around Mount Airy that were involved with his father.

Stockton began using drugs, especially crystal methamphetamine "crank." His career in crime advanced to petty theft with a "weakness for chainsaws." Through the 1960s and 1970s, law enforcement described Stockton this way. "Dennis was a suspect in everything." He started in property crimes such as safe cracking and arson. Then he began to be suspected in unsolved murders and claimed prominent people approached him in murder for hire schemes. One of these Stockton claimed he received a down payment of $2,000 upfront with $3,000 after the kill. It is not a hard stretch to see why law enforcement would not see him as a suspect in the Arnder murder. It is even more difficult that a potential murderer would forgive thousands of dollars for a "hit" that Stockton said never happened. There are many holes in his story, despite what the authors and his lawyers claimed later. When you read the book, you notice many mistakes such as trivial things like the Mayo River running through Kibler Valley, when it is the Dan River. It made me doubt if the authors ever visited the places they were describing. Something that any good documenter of events such as these would do.

Stockton again got out of prison in March 1978. A few months later on July 20, 1978, Kenneth Wayne "Kenny" Arnder was nervous that the police were looking for him because he and another boy were seen stealing some tires. He called Dennis Stockton to get a ride to Kibler Valley to join some friends who were partying. Stockton agreed and picked Kenny up at his mother, Wilma Arnder's, home at 6 p.m. It was the last time she saw her oldest son, one of six.

Stockton claimed he took Arnder to Kibler Valley and then went to deliver some drugs and returned later that same evening.

Arnder told Stockton he was going to stay the night and the latter left him along the Dan River very much alive.

Five days later, Arnder's body was found in Surry County, just south of Mount Airy. He was 17 years old in the summer of 1978, born on October 7, 1959. Arnder's body was shot between the eyes, and his hands were hacked off. Arnder was positioned in a crucifixion position wearing a t-shirt that said, "How Do You Spell Relief—Columbian Gold."

As Stockton was the last person Mrs. Arnder saw her son with, the police naturally questioned him. He remained quiet saying that is the first rule he learned in all those years in a Raleigh prison. Two years later in 1980, he found himself in the Patrick County jail for shooting into the building of a man he said owed him money. Stockton claimed he gave the Patrick County and Surry County sheriffs letters about contract killings he received hoping to put the blame on other people, violating his rule of not snitching on other criminals. Stockton later sued Patrick County in 1984 in a civil case over the conditions of the jail that had been in the same building since before the Civil War.

He wrote later about his time alone in a jail cell. "Laying in a filthy isolation cell all one's life with very little one can do out of lots one needs to do because of the poor lighting one, at times finds himself wondering strange thoughts."

In 1982, Patrick County charged Stockton for the 1978 murder of Arnder believing the killing took place in Kibler Valley that July day the two men left together. It was thought his killing was "contract killing" that cost $1,500 over a "sour drug deal" gone bad. Randy Bowman claimed he was present when Stockton made the deal to kill Arnder, which Stockton denied.

Another man, Robert Gates, testified he was present in June 1979 when Stockton killed another man for "running his mouth." This was Ronnie Tate, who lost his life on July 2-3, 1979, at Stockton's hand in what the latter claimed was self-defense. The story was that Gates, Stockton, and Tate were in Kibler Valley for a swim after attending some dirt track racing. They smoked some "reefer" to calm their nerves as Tate and Gates were wanted men.

Stockton arrived last carrying a gun in the "small of his back" when Tate suddenly drew his pistol on Stockton. Tate reportedly said, "I'm gonna take your money, dope, and car and there's not a damn thing you can do about it. Everyone thinks you're so bad, I wish they could see you now. I'm gonna blow you away, and it won't be the first time I've done it to someone right here." Stockton claimed this was a confession to Arnder's murder and that Tate thought Stockton had put the "cops" on him. At this point, Tate fumbled with his lighter for a cigarette proving smoking kills because at that moment Stockton pulled his gun and fell sideways putting three bullets in Tate, who got one shot off before he "crumpled to the clay."

Gates "frozen in fear" did not move thinking he might be next. Stockton and Gates took Tate to an abandoned Boy Scout Camp in North Carolina, which is eerily similar to what happened to Arnder. Gates could not remember exactly where he and Dennis put Tate's body and other facts in his story were proved not to be true such as that they stopped at the Pinnacle Sandwich Shop, but it was not open that July 4th weekend. Stockton's version of this story tried to show he was not a bad guy, but it backfired on him while he was already in jail in 1982.

Bowman "allegedly" recanted his testimony to Stockton's lawyers, but then denied he did so. Frank Cox testified later that Bowman told him that Bowman lied about Dennis Stockton, but another inmate Cleveland Martin said Bowman would say or do anything if the money was right. Over the years, Stockton's attorneys claimed Bowman changed his story, recanted his story, then signed letters saying he was never made promises about reduced sentences or change of prisons on the threat of perjury charges or other threats from law enforcement.

Later as Stockton's execution approached, three affidavits by Bowman's ex-wife Patricia McHone, a friend of Bowman, Kathy Carreon, and Timothy Crabtree, Bowman's son by McHone stating that Bowman had killed Arnder and bragged about it. Virginia said these were "uncorroborated statements" and refused to help Stockton, who commented that it reminded him of Deuteronomy 17:6 "At the mouth of two witnesses, or three witnesses, shall he that is worthy of death be put to death; but at the mouth of one witness he shall not be put to death."

During the first trial in August 1982, law enforcement carried Bowman from Surry County to Patrick County across the state line. There were insinuations that Bowman received a deal as 17 days after the trial, charges against him for obtaining stolen property in North Carolina were dropped. Anthony Giorno, the Virginia prosecutor, said, "People ask us for stuff all the time. We can't promise you anything." North Carolina refused to prosecute McBride in 1983 on charges of conspiracy to commit capital murder even though Virginia sent evidence to them.

The book on Stockton reported that several times the hands were knocked off the angel on his tombstone, but when this author visited his grave at Oakdale Cemetery in Mount Airy, there was no angel only a set of hands praying lying flat on the tombstone. The authors claimed this was an intimidation tactic from the real killers.

Stockton's attorneys in their attempts to get him a new trial or stay of execution and the authors of his book spoke openly about police corruption in Patrick and Surry Counties respectively. The book claims that a Patrick County officer, Bob Day, visited Stockton in prison looking for dirty on lead investigator Jay Gregory, a friend of this author and his family. The visitor told Stockton supposedly that there was evidence that the killing did not take place in Virginia, which made the conviction and death sentence a moot point. Gregory, the book claims, used the Stockton conviction to win an election for Sheriff of Patrick County.

Patrick County politics is well known for the cliquish nature of its politics. Tom Joyce of the *Mount Airy News*, who comes from Patrick County as well had some choice comments in the book about Stockton saying. "Stuart is a different world than Mount Airy. People there don't question authority...If [Officials] say something's true, it must be." The Mount Airy News thought Stockton was innocent and some at the newspaper received death threats for taking that stance in the case, via editorials. The book describes Patrick County as the place where the southside meets the Blue Ridge Mountains and ruled by a wealthy few, who got that way via tobacco and wood. It says that the "byzantine Patrick County politics" sacrifice "justice for the sake of careers."

Stockton was Patrick County's first death penalty conviction of the twentieth century and the book claims that it propelled the careers of prosecutor Anthony Giorno and investigator Jay Gregory, who won election for Commonwealth Attorney (Virginia's version of District Attorney) and Sheriff, respectively.

Giorno was contacted about this chapter but declined to participate. However, he was reported saying the following on July 6, 1994, about an accusation that he hid evidence to convict an innocent man. "It's repugnant to suggest that I would use tainted evidence that would lead an innocent man to death row. I am convinced I did nothing wrong."

In 1987, a Federal Judge vacated Stockton's death sentence due what he considered a "tainted jury." A diner operator in Stuart, where the jury was eating told them that Stockton should be executed. The judge gave Stockton a choice of new sentencing or a life term. Stockton could have saved his life by choosing the latter, but he went with a new sentencing hearing and was again given the death sentence.

In 1989, Stockton's attorneys filed affidavits from former Patrick County Deputy Clifford Boyd and former Sheriff Jesse Williams, who Gregory defeated in an election after the Stockton trial. They claimed Bowman was still angry because Gregory and Surry County authorities promised to transfer to another prison and a reduced sentence. Bowman said he was promised he would not be sent back to North Carolina.

Stockton began keeping a diary of his prison time in 1983 up through his death. Like many inmates facing death, Dennis Stockton found God and was baptized on March 1, 1991. Three Virginia Governors, Democrat and Republican, Chuck Robb, Douglas Wilder, and George Allen all reviewed Stockton's sentence and declined to act.

As his time approached, Stockton began publishing stories in the Norfolk newspaper. Virginia moved Stockton from the Mecklenburg County Correctional Facility, where he had been involved in a potential break out of "Death Row," but he did not leave the prison, on September 16, 1995, to Greensville, Virginia. One of his lawyers made a joke with Stockton on his last day as the inmate smoked his last Marlboro in his orange jumpsuit while drinking a Coke, telling him, "Don't smoke that, it'll kill you."

On September 27, 1995, Virginia put its 27th inmate in two decades to death via lethal injection. Dennis Waldon Stockton had a choice of that or electrocution. Being a former drug addict, he chose the needle. He told the prison officials that "I know you're just doing your jobs." In what was described as a "cruel joke," the phone in the death chamber rang twice giving hope to Stockton that he might be saved from death. Virginia, being the oldest "political jurisdiction" in America being settled starting in 1607 has executed more felons than any other state.

Wilma Arnder was there that day and watched Stockton strapped on the gurney to receive his death sentence. She always thought Dennis Stockton killed her son even though he called her after Kenny disappeared and after the body was discovered.

Friends of Stockton reportedly took his ashes up on the Blue Ridge Mountains and spread them in a waterfall that went into the James River, but if it was anywhere near Mount Airy, the ashes would have flowed into the Yadkin or maybe more appropriately into the Dan River. Considering the book on Stockton many mistakes, one must wonder.

After Stockton's execution, the case did not die. In 1996, Randy Bowman asked for $1,000 to tell the "real story," but no American media outlets were interested. In 2000, William Shaw of High Point, North Carolina, claimed Arnder was killed in a small house on the outskirts of Mount Airy after he was tied up and tortured.

Kibler Valley along the Dan River near the site, where Arnder's body was found.

Above, the grave of Kenneth Arnder at Oakdale Cemetery in Mount Airy. Below, Dennis Stockton on death row in Virginia.

16 EXTRA PAGES IN THIS ISSUE!

INSIDE detective

EVERY STORY TRUE

FEBRUARY

10¢

Virginia's
HONEYMOON DEATH RIDDLE

SOLVING ARIZONA'S NIGHT CLUB SLAYING

Inside Detective Magazine from 1937 tells the story of the murder at Mount Airy Knitting, later Spencer's Knitting Company.

Chapter Twelve:

<u>MURDER AT MOUNT AIRY KNITTING</u>

There was once a time in this nation before television that many got their information about true crime from magazines. Today, as magazines and newspapers die out due to the growth of the internet, it is good to look back to the past at these publications. Most of these magazines published sensationalized and scintillating stories with little adherence to the truth, but occasionally, you stumble on to a reliable source. Such is the subject of this chapter. Written by Mount Airy Police Officer J. Willis Jessup from the February 1937 issue of *Inside Detective* magazine edited by West F. Peterson.

It really was a dark rainy night in Mount Airy, North Carolina, the last night of November 1934. A terrific thunderstorm rolled over the town that night as Goble Hawks, and Buck Gwyn were working in the dye house of Mount Airy Knitting Company. The two men were alone in the factory except for William Phillips, who had two jobs as a fireman for the boiler and as a night watchman. At 11 p.m., Phillips made his way around the plant to make his rounds as the latter.

Lightning, rain, and howling wind were outside the factory located near the intersection of Oak and Willow Streets, a block away from Main Street. Hawks and Gwyn decided to eat their lunch on the late shift in the basement at the end of the building. Suddenly, a loud crash echoed through the building, but the two men ignored it.

When they returned to work the water in the dye vats was getting cold. They thought Phillips must have let the fire in the boiler go down to eat lunch too. Hawks walked to the boiler room to investigate and came back quickly to inform Gwyn that Phillips was dead, murdered.

A few minutes later Hawks, "coatless and hatless" rushed into the Mount Airy Police Department at 11:55 p.m. Officer J. Willis Jessup went ahead to the mill. Jessup found the whitewashed walls of the boiler room "splattered in blood" and

Phillips in the back of the room, dead in his overalls with blood dripping from his still warm body.

Jessup notified Surry County Sheriff J. D. Thompson and Coroner Dr. R. J. Lovall, who soon arrived at the scene. They found Phillips received a fatal shot from a large caliber pistol above the heart in a downward direction that exited out his right kidney and another shot that went through his left leg. The officers found the bullets near the coal pile that fueled the boiler and another in a pine chair that sat in the room.

Law enforcement questioned Hawks and Gwyn and gleaned that Phillips, age 52, was last seen at 11:20 p.m. and the other two men were together the entire time until 11:45 p.m. when Hawks went in search of Phillips. Neither man claimed to hear a gunshot due to the storm raging outside the mill. The investigation ruled out robbery as November 30, 1934, was payday and Phillips still had his pay envelope full of money and his watch. Officers noted that the killer knew the layout of the mill as the entrance to the boiler room from outside was a "circuitous route" through a narrow and dark alley, which a stranger would never discover, and that the last fifty feet would have been in plain view of Phillips acting as fireman.

Mount Airy Police Chief R. E. Lawrence along with Sheriff Thompson and Deputy Harvey Boyd began interviewing the five hundred employees of Mount Airy Knitting Company, men, and women, but no good leads came from the attempt. The only evidence was the two .38 caliber bullets fired from a Smith and Wesson revolver.

Officer Jessup, who wrote the magazine article, engaged three men he trusted, who worked at the plant in three separate departments, to ask around casually about who owned pistols, but everyone owned a gun and tests on all those weapons met with no matches to the murder weapon.

The case went cold, but then Cager Phillips, brother of the victim took it upon himself to investigate and brought in a .38 caliber Smith and Wesson that he believed was the gun that killed his brother. The weapon in question belonged to Gabe McCraw, who lived in the "Cattis Hill" section of Surry County, North Carolina.

Gabe McCraw, described as a "young married man of fair reputation" denied owning a gun when questioned earlier in the case. Cager Phillips got McCraw to sell him the gun. The gun was sent to the FBI after an initial local test indicated it might be the murder weapon.

Chief Lawrence brought McCraw in for questioning. The article tells the scene this way. "A brawny, handsome young man...walked into our presence with the air of a person with a clear conscience, but there was a spark of resentment in his cold blue eyes." McCraw stated his father borrowed the gun in question Labor Day to kill a cat.

McCraw's wife, Shirley, described as "barely out of her teens" said that her husband was with her all night of the murder. She claimed they went to a movie and were home before the storm in bed. She swore six different people would swear that Gabe McCraw was home including her brother, Hurley Holder.

Law enforcement brought in Holder for questioning describing him as a "typical underworld type, weak face, receding chin, and a pair of shifty gray eyes that were strangely repellent."

Holder "nervously" claimed he knew nothing, but it was felt he was not telling the truth as his own alibi kept changing. Chief Lawrence grilled Holder and told him not to leave the area.

Shirley allowed Chief Lawrence to look around the house and he found two exploded .38 caliber shells hidden in a flue base for a wood stove under a tin cap that was obviously tampered with that Lawrence thought was a feeble attempt to hide the shiny shells. Lawrence stated it was an "odd place to find empty shells" and that the shells had not been there long as they were so clean.

The FBI report said that "it is highly probable that the gun in question fired the enclosed bullet, but this department cannot be absolutely positive." Police returned the gun to McCraw, who was reportedly "arrogant" about the situation. He thought he had gotten away with murder.

McCraw did not realize that his brother-in-law was still a loose gun. On August 31, 1935, nine months after the murder, Hurley Holder found himself at Check's Road House, three miles south of Mount Airy. Described as "eyes somewhat glazed with liquor," Holder found his date at the establishment dancing with another man. When confronted, the other man claimed to have known the girl for years, but Holder caused a scene and was drug from Check's raving that he was not a coward and would kill the other man. He stated "I killed one man and I'll kill another. I killed old man Phillips." Friends drove him home that night and Holder thought the incident was forgotten, but he was wrong.

Ten days later, Hugh Barlow, went to the Mount Airy Police Department and told what happened that night at Check's. He claimed he was reluctant to tell the story out of friendship with Holder, but his conscience led him to tell the story thinking that the Phillips family deserved justice for what happened to who Barlow thought was an innocent man.

On September 10, 1935, Officers C. F. Melton and the author of the magazine story, J. Willis Jessup, quietly arrested Holder at Fred Jarrell's gas station. They described Holder as seeming to be expecting it.

Under questioning, Holder claimed the murder was an accident. He told that his brother-in-law, Gabe McCraw, and he planned to rob Goble Hawks that night on payday because it was known that Hawks "carried a roll." Holder spent that night at his sister's home, but they snuck out when she fell asleep. They claimed they thought it was Phillips' night off work and that Goble would be in the boiler room.

Holder said he and McCraw heard Phillips shoveling coal. Holder said he was supposed to hit Phillips, whom they thought was Hawks with an iron pipe to knock him out, but Phillips heard them. Holder said McCraw told Phillips to "Throw up your hands." Phillips responded by using his shovel as a weapon knocking the pipe out of Holder's hands and then went for McCraw, who shot him. Holder claimed he was trying to recover his pipe and did not hear the gunshot due to the noise of the boiler and storm outside, which he described as "terrific by that time."

The two murderers ran out of the mill with McCraw leading the way through the downpour of the still raging storm down Willow Street and plunged into a creek on their way home. They arrived completely drenched and found Shirley awake, but she did not ask where they had been.

M. F. Patterson arrested Gabe McCraw the next morning, but he made no statement except to deny his involvement in the crime. Next came the trials for both men.

On October 2, 1935, Holder pleaded guilty in Surry County Superior Court to second-degree murder in a deal with Solicitor Allen H. Gwyn. Judge J. S. Rousseau sentenced Holder to 25 to 30 years in prison. Attorney Edward C. Bivens represented Gabe McCraw and got a continuance for his client.

Whatever happened in the meantime is not known, but on January 6, 1936, from his cell at the Cary State Penal Farm in Wake County, North Carolina, Holder reversed his statement. He claimed he alone did the robbery and murder. On February 20, 1936, the court convicted McCraw as an accessory after the fact and received two to four years as Holder refused to testify against his brother-in-law claiming again that he was no coward. It seems to this author that the person who was not a coward in this story of true crime was night watchman William Phillips, who fought for life.

Mount Airy Knitting Company became Spencer's and made children's clothes for decades. My grandparents came to Mount Airy about a decade later from Chattanooga, Tennessee, to work in the textile mills bringing my then teenage father with them. He worked in this same mill as a young man before going off to college to be a real student athlete at Lees-McCrae and Appalachian State Teacher's College, now a university.

Today, years after the plant closed, the City of Mount Airy is working to turn the former factory into a place to live and be entertained by bringing more people to downtown Mount Airy long after the murder in the mill occurred.

Today it is an empty factory that is a hot topic for renovation, but there was a time that Spencer's, formerly Mount Airy Knitting was the scene of a murder.

264

Goble Hawks was the intended victim at Mount Airy Knitting instead of William Phillips.

C. F. Melton

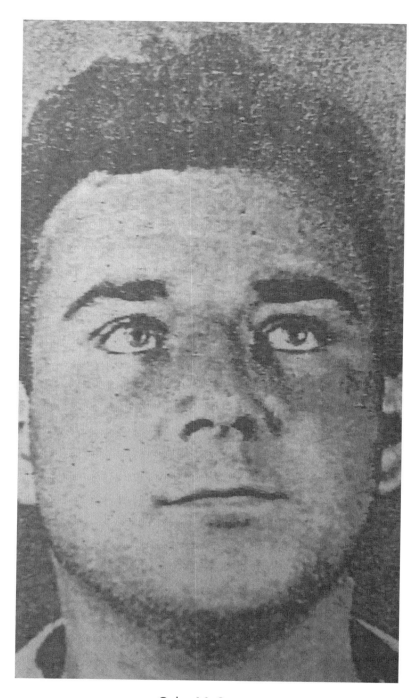

Gabe McCraw

Mount Airy Police Chief R. E. Lawrence.

Above, Mount Airy Knitting Company on Willow Street.
Below, Check's Road House.

J. Willis Jessup, a ballistics expert with the Mount Airy Police,
wrote the story for *Inside Detective*.

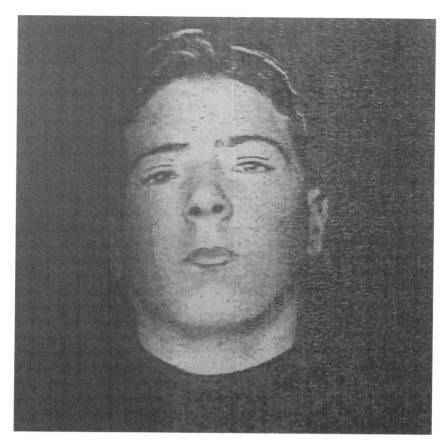

Hurley Holder

"That's A Damn Good Dog!"

COMMONWEALTH OF VIRGINIA
VS.
STEPHEN MATTESON EPPERLY
(1980) A RETROSPECTIVE

ROYCE GLENNWOOD
LOOKABILL

Woody Lookabill's book on the Epperly/Hall Murder.

Chapter Thirteen:

<u>WHERE IS GINA HALL?</u>

In the summer of 2016, Scentsy brought me one of the bestselling books I ever published. Kathy Kiser Valencic, who sells the very good smelling wax and burners to release many fragrances into the world. She worked with the Montgomery County, Virginia, parole department and told me of a Judge who needed his book published. Later that year, I spent many days with Judge Royce Woodrow "Woody" Lookabill selling his book "That's A Damn Good Dog!" that I published about the murder case of Gina Hall and the conviction of Steve Epperly, who was Lookabill's client back in 1980.

Many did not realize that Woody and his partner, David Warburton, were appointed to represent Epperly by Judge Arthur Chambers in a trial that began in December 1980. The attorneys had no choice in the matter. There were no public defenders at that time in Pulaski County, Virginia.

Over the course of that summer of 2016, we heard many theories and stories relating to the case. I think Woody was glad he lost the case as Epperly was the first person convicted in Virginia without a body, but it left another thought in all our minds. Where is Gina Hall?

In the fall of 1981, I began attending Virginia Tech after two years at Surry Community College in Dobson, North Carolina. On many Friday nights to blow off steam, I found myself at the "Happy Hour" at the Marriott Hotel. I vaguely remember hearing about the case, but with the pounding of Michael Jackson on the dance floor, murder was a far-removed thought in my mind. Like many Hokies, I liked to dance with Radford Coeds.

On Saturday, June 29, 1980, a Radford girl, Gina Renee Hall, age 18, had just finished her first year at the school where my father got his master's degree. Hall was at the Marriott Four Seasons Hotel to dance. She liked to dance and was very athletic. As a young girl, Gina had been burned and was self-conscious about scar tissue on her body. She was not a girl who normally picked up guys at bars, but she was celebrating.

That night, Gina Hall met Steve Epperly. He was a 28-year-old former Virginia Tech football player. He was in great physical shape known for his weightlifting and the ability to bench press.

He worked in various jobs such as substitute teaching and on the grounds crew at Radford University. Epperly was with a friend, who had access to a Claytor Lake house. Hall agreed to go with Epperly believing that others were going to join them. They left in Hall's Chevy. She was never seen again.

There was a dark side to Epperly. Previously charged twice for sexual assault, but since he had a prior consensual relationship with one of the victims that case was dismissed. He had been physically abusive to his family specifically to his mother and father. He was known to have road rage incidents such as pulling strangers out of cars and beating them up for no apparent reason. There were stories about abusing animals as a young man. He was a classic textbook case for a potential serial killer. There are rumors about another girl before Gina Hall, who disappeared in the Richmond area after a relationship with Epperly.

Later that night and the next day, Epperly's friend saw and heard him in the house. He was seen downstairs, shirtless, cleaning up using a towel that was later found with Gina Hall's folded clothes on the Radford side under a tree on the banks of the New River. That towel was given to a tracking dog to sniff outside the

Radford Police Department. When the dog entered the station, it walked up to Steve Epperly.

While no one saw Gina Hall after leaving the Marriott, someone did talk to her. Gina called her sister, Diana, from the lake house telling her she was with a guy named Steve. Epperly claimed that Hall drove him back to his home in Radford.

On June 30, a two-tone brown Chevrolet Monte Carlo belonging to Gina Hall was found near the train trestle on Hazel Hollow Road in Radford. The driver's seat was pushed as far back as possible. Certainly, more likely to be for the tall Epperly than the barely five-foot Hall.

In the summer of 2016, I heard many stories, and this chapter is my viewpoint and does not reflect the view of Woody Lookabill or anyone else involved in the case. One of the most chilling came from a lady, who dated Epperly before the disappearance of Gina Hall. She told us that she was very glad she did not say "NO" to Epperly, or she might have been another victim.

On September 8, 1980, the Grand Jury of Pulaski County indicted Stephen Matterson Epperly for the murder of Gina Renee Hall. The trial began in December 1980.

During the trial, the journey of a tracking dog named Harass II was described. This dog did a remarkable thing ten days after Gina Hall's disappearance. Harass went from the site where Hall's car was found across the trestle into Radford, through a car wash and stopped at Steve Epperly's front door. The rain enhanced the dog's ability to track Epperly's scent. During the trial, Epperly exclaimed aloud, "That's a damn good dog."

While many think the dog convicted Epperly, it was the testimony of Virginia State Trooper C. Austin Hall that did the real damage along with Epperly himself. During the investigation, Epperly had gone to the office of Blacksburg businessman Bill Cranwell. He asked Cranwell to his ask his brother, Attorney Richard Cranwell if they could convict him without a body. What Epperly did not know was that Cranwell's roommate at Virginia Tech years earlier was John Hall, the father of Gina Hall.

Steve Epperly did not testify at his trial. He did ask the judge if he could fire his lawyers, falsely believing it would cause a mistrial. You get the feeling he thought he was smarter than those involved in the legal profession. The jury returned a guilty verdict for first-degree murder on December 16, 1980. Three days later, Judge Arthur sentenced Epperly to life in prison.

Attorneys offered Epperly a plea deal of 25 years for second-degree murder but refused it claiming he was innocent. He would have been released in the early 2000s or earlier and would have been a free man for twenty years assuming no persons went missing with contact to him. It became clear to me in the summer of 2016 that Steve Epperly had the makings of a serial killer and I doubt Gina Hall would have been the only girl to fall victim to him. Epperly now lives in the Buckingham County Corrections Facility run by the Commonwealth of Virginia, and I doubt if he will ever see the light of day as a free man again.

Lookabill and Warburton received $400 for three months work in the case that I expect both were glad they lost, but where is Gina Hall? Many people presented theories to us that summer and here are some of them.

One fisherman reported that night that he heard a motorboat engine that started near the house, where Epperly was seen. The boat faded out of sound in the distance and then returned an hour later leading the fisherman to believe Epperly took Hall's body down the lake away from the dam and disposed of it. Police searched the lake thoroughly but found nothing.

Another theory was that he dropped her body in a passing coal train, that no one noticed it, and her body was taken far away and incinerated with the coal. The problem I had with this theory was if you visit the trestle, there is nowhere he could have gotten above the tracks high enough to drop her body into a passing coal car.

A former brother-in-law of Epperly told us he thought Epperly took the body to land in Craig County and buried her there. This trip one way would be over an hour if he dared take Interstate 81 or more like an hour and a half going the back way via 114 to 460 to 42. If he took the less traveled route, it would have meant three hours driving time and then the time it took to get rid of the body. The former brother-in-law told me Epperly is "Where he needs to be."

Another theory states that Epperly took her to two different incinerators in the Radford area including one at St. Albans, the former boy's school, and mental hospital. Another theory states that Epperly buried Hall in the foundation at St. Albans as his job was to spread gravel in the pits there during construction. Police found Hall's car very close to St. Albans on Hazel Hollow Road. Many paranormal investigators claim that Gina Hall's spirit still exists at St. Albans and even television programs have been produced reporting this theory including *The Dead Files* in 2014 on the Travel Channel.

The theory that gets the most mentions is that since Epperly worked at Radford University on the grounds crew, he knew about construction at the Deadmon Center. Sounding like Jimmy Hoffa being placed in wet concrete at Giant's Stadium in New Jersey, that Gina Hall's body was placed in the foundation of the Deadmon Center.

One person who has not given up on finding Gina Hall is Radford City Police Department Lt. Andy Wilburn. He has heard of some of the locations such as Epperly may have hidden Hall's body include under the Deadmon Center at Radford University and at other construction sites. Wilburn has heard Gina Hall is in Claytor Lake, the New River, buried beside Interstate 81 and under a coffin in another person's grave. He has also been told that her body was placed on a train and in another state. He has heard that Epperly ground up her body at the asphalt plant and is in the road or that she was incinerated. He says, "Everybody's got a theory, but unless you can analyze all of the data, it's not an educated theory, it's just a guess," he points out. "I've had people call me who have had dreams and visions. I'm looking at it based on facts and circumstances from that night and the next day." If you have any information about the location of Gina Hall's body, please contact Andy Wilburn at Andy.Wilburn@radfordva.gov or (540) 267-3201. Another group that I discovered in writing this book was Help Save The Next Girl, which was founded after the abduction and murder of a Virginia Tech student in 2009. "Help Save The Next Girl's primary focus is to spread safety information and prevent future crimes against young women. This can be accomplished through maintaining vigilance and personal awareness. As a community, we must know our neighbors, be responsible for one another, and cherish precious family." The organization has chapters in colleges and universities, middle and high schools including Virginia Tech and Radford.

Gina Hall

http://helpsavethenextgirl.com/

Photos of Steve Epperly are few and hard to find.

Above, the Epperly home in Radford, Virginia.
Below, the house where the murder took place on Claytor Lake.

The trestle where the dog walked across and under which Gina Hall's car was found on the New River at Radford, Virginia.

Woody Lookabill along the New River on Hazel Hollow Road.

Above, St. Albans Sanatorium, where many believe Gina Hall's spirit resides. Below, Pulaski County Courthouse held the trial.

The home of Floyd Allen at the base of Fancy Gap, Virginia.

Chapter Fourteen:

"TWO SIDES TO THE STORY" THE HILLSVILLE SHOOTOUT

Over the years doing book events there is one question I always get. "Do you have anything about the Hillsville shootout?" Well, now that question will be in the affirmative. Hillsville has come to be synonymous with the massacre of six people and still a very controversial subject. It has become the subject of myth and legends even more with the advent of the internet and social media.

The two "warring sides" included the Allens, who were wealthy Democrats in a county dominated by the Republicans. Someone said of the Carroll County Court House Clique. "It doesn't make any difference what the evidence is, the case goes the way they want it to go."

Next door in Patrick County, where I grew up there was a courthouse clique that was Democrat, while most of the people in the rural county were conservatives and voted Republican, especially for President. My family has been the victim of the Stuart Court House Clique, but I did not go shoot all the

Democrats. There are certain lines that civilized persons do not cross.

The other thing I have learned about the Hillsville Shootout is that "just because Grandma said, it does not mean it is true." Adding to over a dozen books about the shootout, the following chapter is my take on the most famous true crime story of our region. It involves a love triangle, politics, and pride, lots of pride. "Pride cometh before a fall." Many people died because Floyd Allen did not realize that his refusal to go to jail would do to the lives of so many people.

Floyd Allen, born in 1857, was the fourth generation in Carroll County when Floyd and his brothers, Sidna, Anderson, Victor, Garland, Washington, and Jasper Allen came of age. Someone who knew Floyd described him as carrying "himself erect, went well, and appropriately dressed at home or in public, was exceedingly polite and courteous to everyone he considered his friend." Someone who did not know Floyd described him as "a clan leader, who were 'satisfactory citizens' when the breeze blew to suit them...but the moment it turned, they were fire-eyed demons." Described as "your best friend or your worst enemy," Floyd once shot his own brother, Jack. Floyd was a vain man, who kept his mustache neatly trimmed and always carried a comb and a toothbrush in his shirt pocket.

The Allens involved in the shootout came from Jeremiah Allen (1825-97), who married Nancy Combs. Jeremiah's father was Carr Allen, who descended from William and William Allen, Jr., the latter fought in the American Revolution.

Carroll County started in 1842, carved from Grayson and Patrick Counties. In 1888, the railroad came ten miles away in Sylvatus and twenty-five miles away in Mount Airy, North Carolina. Children went to school when not raising crops. Churches included everything from Primitive Baptist to Presbyterians including Reverend Robert Childress, "The Man Who Moved A Mountain." Childress blamed the uptick in violence on the Primitive Baptists, "a sub-denomination that sprouted like mushrooms from the dark corners of every hollow and cove." The Allens were Primitive Baptists.

In 1893, a financial collapse sent the area into an era of violence. Murders rose to thirty in the twenty years from 1890 until 1910. The previous twenty years only saw four crimes. One man named Webb said, "I thought I was justified in what I did." He said that just before they hung him in Carroll County for the murder of his father-in-law, something many of us have contemplated. The majority rule of Carroll County switched from Democrat to Republican around 1890.

Sidna Allen had been back in Carroll County nine months when the trouble began. He was a successful businessman, who had invested in real estate and taught school. He went to the Klondike in Alaska to search for gold in 1898. He traveled to Hawaii and the western United States.

Ten years later, he built his "Dream Home" of the best timber that he kiln dried and dressed. It had eight rooms with running water and gas-powered lights. Built in 1911, Sidna's "Queen Anne and Carpenter Gothic Style" house has been described as the "most beautiful home in Carroll County" was only his home for a year. In 1912, Sidna owned over 1,000 acres of land. He was 5' 9" tall and was 48 years old at the time of the trial. Married to Betty Mitchell in 1901, they had two daughters and operated a store that is no longer standing across the road from his house.

On Saturday, December 17, 1910, a corn shucking hosted by Herbert Easter, who was married to Cornelia Allen, sister of Floyd and Sidna Allen, until her death in 1903, became the catalyst that all the events hereafter discussed. Wesley Edwards found a red ear of corn and was the "custom," he got to kiss the girl of his choosing. He chose Rachel McCraw, the girlfriend or the "intended" of William Thomas.

William Sidna Edwards was one of nine children. Single and known to be a moonshiner, he was six-foot-tall and age 23 at the time of the shootout. His fellow moonshiner and brother, Wesley Victor Edwards, was 5' 7" and age 21, known to have "little guy syndrome," with a smart mouth and prone to fight at the drop of a hat. His girlfriend was Maude Iroler, who would have an enormous impact on the outcome of the events about to unfold.

On December 18, several men arrived outside Flint Hill School, where church services were underway. Garland Allen, brother of Floyd, was preaching that day. Led by William Thomas, George Thomas, Bud Edwards, and Homer Leftwich were looking for Wesley Edwards and trouble over the corn shucking the night before. The adversaries exchanged words, and Sidna Edwards came to his brother's defense. There are legends of gunfire and the different sides throwing rocks at the church service.

Indictments came down against the Edwards brothers for a misdemeanor in 1911 for disturbing public worship, but not for William Thomas and others. The two Edwards brothers left for North Carolina to work at the granite quarry in Mount Airy for about four months

Many believe this "ruckus" was an opportunity for Carroll County Commonwealth Attorney, the district attorney in other parts of the country, William McDonald Foster, to get even with the Allens. Foster, age 44 at the time of the shootout, was "carrying water on both shoulders, "a term for a Democrat turned

Republican, just to get elected in the county. Married to the former Katherine Tipton, Foster had five children.

Bad blood between Foster and the Allens was complex. Foster defeated Jack Allen's son, Walter, to become Commonwealth Attorney in 1907. His trouble with Floyd Allen went back to an incident regarding a North Carolina prosecution of a man named "Cody," who took a shot at Floyd. Allen threatened to kill Foster over the interference.

There was bad blood between Dexter Goad and Floyd Allen too. Floyd Allen said, "There was never an opportunity that Dexter Goad had to do me wrong that he did not do it."

In 1902, Dexter Goad, a U. S. Commissioner resigned his position after Floyd Allen reported him for selling "blockade liquor" in his offices. Goad, age 45, at the time of shootout was married to Martha Quesenberry and had eight children. Known for wearing a black cape and a bowler hat, Goad served in the legislature previously.

Dexter Goad, a Republican, became Carroll County Clerk of Court in 1905. Floyd Allen petitioned the court charging Goad with creating false returns. Goad countered with his own petition. This election was the end of Democrats in Carroll County. Goad accused Floyd Allen of lying about an expense report involving transport of prisoners from Wytheville. Allen said that he would vote for a pig before he voted for Goad because he had pigs smarter than Goad. The Allens served in various political positions in Carroll County. In 1883, Jeremiah was the Fancy Gap Supervisor. Two years later, Jack was a Constable for Fancy Gap. Floyd served as Supervisor in the late 1890s. In 1911, Carroll County elected Goad, Foster, and a new Sheriff, Lewis Franklin Webb, to office. Webb, age 64, was married to Nancy Mullins and had eleven children. He lost the previous election and served as a deputy.

The Allens considered all of them political enemies. Sidna Allen said later that the "little courthouse ring of Republicans, who hated us bitterly and with us out of the way it would be easier for them to run things."

Surry County Sheriff Cabell Haynes and Deputy Oscar Monday, a step-brother of the Edwards brothers arrested the two

Edwards boys on April 10, 1911, by. They were delivered to the state line. There is no record of proper extradition papers being filed. Carroll County Deputy Thomas "Pinky" Samuels was sent with a buggy that carried only two people. Samuels deputized Peter Easter, who had a buggy that carried four people. Wesley was handcuffed, and Sidna Edwards was tied in the four-person buggy for transport back to Hillsville.

The deputies chose to take the two fugitives by the home of their uncle, Floyd Allen. They had other choices leading many to believe it was deliberate, just as the indictments being only for the Edwards boys led many to believe it was part of a setup. There were three roads including Ward's Gap, but they chose the worst road at that time, Fancy Gap, which passed by the homes five Allen brothers Floyd, SIdna, Victor, Garland, and Jasper "Jack." Easter warned Samuels about the choice, but "Pinky" replied that a law officer could go anywhere he pleased.

On this Thursday, Floyd Allen confronted the deputies near his brother, Sidna's house, at the top of Fancy Gap about the way his nephews were being treated. Floyd was "irate at seeing his nephews humiliated and shackled because of a misdemeanor."

Since their father's death, Floyd projected a "father figure"

towards them. Their mother, Alverta Allen, married John J.

Edwards, but he died in 1903. Floyd felt they should be taken to

jail like "men, not animals." Sidna, Jackson, and Barnett Allen saw

the altercation.

Deputy "Pinky" Samuels drew his pistol on Floyd, but he

managed to take the weapon away from the deputy, broke it over

a rock, and then struck Samuels with the weapon. Floyd promised

to bring the boys to Hillsville on Monday himself in a more

humane manner.

True to his word, Floyd arrived with his nephews, who

received a magistrate's trial. Wesley Edwards served sixty days for

disturbing a public worship service, and Sidney served thirty days

for the same charge. Their "punishment" involved worked in

Sheriff Joe Blankenship's orchard during the day and going home

overnight. Thomas and the others involved were never charged.

Deputy Samuels filed charges against Floyd for "maiming,

assault, and rescue of prisoners." In an unusual occurrence, Floyd appeared before the Grand Jury himself. The jury indicted Floyd, and a trial date of June 1911 was set. Trials occurred four times a year at that time.

Floyd, six-foot-tall, and 58 years old at the time of his trial was a merchant known as "ruthless" in his business practices. His store sat in the adjoining yard of his home at the base of Fancy Gap. When Carroll County officials needed a "tough job" completed, Floyd was the man they called.

In June 1911, Deputy Samuels was a no-show. Apparently, Jack Allen confronted him, and he never came back to Carroll County. There were not enough witnesses present to continue Floyd's trial. The trial was postponed until March 1912, the next court date. One story is that John Moore approached Floyd and told him if he supported Dexter Goad for Clerk of Court in the next election, the jury would acquit. Floyd refused saying he "did not sell himself in that way."

Sheriff Joe Blankenship went out of office at the beginning of 1912. He warned Judge Massie that Floyd Allen might not take a sentence of jail time well. Floyd shot Noah Combs in 1904 over a real estate deal when a bullet bounced off a wood stove in a wagon and into Comb's leg. Sentenced to one hour and $100, Floyd refused to serve or pay and got a pardon from the Governor of Virginia. Clearly in the wrong, Floyd Allen thought he was above the law of the Commonwealth of Virginia. Lewis Webb, age 64, won election as Sheriff of Carroll County. Massie ignored the warnings and refused to disarm people in his courtroom saying, "he was there to prosecute, not persecute."

Judge Thornton Lemmon Massie was 46 at the time and had served on the 21st Circuit Court since 1908. Massie was married with three children and lived in Pulaski, Virginia. He had lost his left hand as a young man.

In 1912, anyone could carry a gun out in the open. Only law enforcement and, mail carriers could carry concealed weapons. On the day of the shootout, it seemed everyone was "packing heat." All the Allens including Floyd, who could carry concealed as a "special policeman," except Victor, who was a mail carrier, were carrying. Victor Allen, age 30 at the time of the shootout was married to Emma Wisler and had three children.

On Tuesday, March 12, 1912, Judge Massie convened the trial after lunch. There were twenty-one witnesses, but still no "Pinky" Samuels. Foster in excessive hyperbole told the jury to "take courage and do their duty in relieving the county of mob violence, which had reigned for fifteen or twenty years." Judge Massie adjourned court the next day at 2 p.m. The jury stayed overnight in the Texas House Hotel.

On the night of March 13, Floyd stayed at his brother, Sidna's home at the top of Fancy Gap, south of Hillsville, instead of traveling the fifteen miles below the mountain to his home. He would not return to his house until his casket arrived for his funeral.

It rained all night making the roads nearly impassable. Described as "raw, wet, and cold," Thursday, March 14, 1912, was not a pleasant day weather wise and would soon turn even more gloomy. Floyd came in with his attorneys Walter S. Tipton and David W. Bolen wearing a dark suit and a red/gray sweater. His sandy hair was graying, but his blue-gray eyes still garnered attention when leveled at you.

Court started earlier than usual at eight and a half hour later, the jury reached a guilty verdict and a sentence of one year in prison and no fine. Foreman Charley Howell read the verdict that Floyd was guilty of assault and illegal rescue. Floyd's attorney, David Bolen, asked for and received a motion to hear an appeal. Judge Massie set a hearing for the next morning. Bolen asked for bond for Floyd Allen, but it was denied by Judge Massie. The judge ordered Floyd Allen taken into custody.

Floyd Allen, although arrested many times, had never spent time in jail and had vowed he never would. "Floyd was to be in the hands of his enemies, who would humiliate him and his people by incarcerating him in the county jail." Floyd Allen pronounced, "Gentlemen, I just ain't agoin."

Sheriff Lewis Webb stepped forward and instructed Deputy Elihu Gillespie, "Take hold of him" referring to Floyd Allen. Webb reached behind his back to get handcuffs. Floyd said later he thought Webb was going for his gun. Ron Hall in his book on the shootout believes that Sheriff Webb fired the first shot, but he may have been fumbling with a gun he was not familiar with as he had just borrowed the .38 caliber pistol expecting there might be trouble in the courtroom that day. It might have gone off accidentally.

If we could stop time and observe the courtroom at this moment, the reader would see the courtroom was twenty feet smaller than it is today. From the back of the room near the doors, you would see Judge Massie on the far wall with Clerk of Court Dexter Goad on the judge's left, the viewer's right. The jury sat in front of the judge at a lower level. Sheriff Webb sat below Goad facing Foster with deputies to their left, your right. Floyd Allen sat on the viewer's left, the judge's right with spectators behind Allen. On the viewer's far left, parallel with Judge Massie sat Sidna and Claude Allen. Claude, age 22 was six-foot-tall and engaged to Nellie Wisler. He was known as a banjo player, who took very good care of his mother.

On the viewer's near right sat Wesley Edwards with Victor Allen. Sidna Edwards sat in the back left and Friel Allen on the back right as the viewer saw the courtroom. Friel was Jack Allen's son at age 20, 5' 9" tall, was single and reportedly the best shot in

Carroll County. The participants were lined up for a proverbial shootout.

As the deputy tried to take Floyd Allen into custody, all hell broke loose in the Carroll County Court House. Whether it was a gunshot or an accidental spark going off in the wood stove, nothing was ever the same again for the Allens or the history of Hillsville.

Floyd Allen later testified that Dexter Goad pulled a pistol from behind his back, which was not proven, and aimed at him. Floyd thought that Goad winked at Sheriff Webb in an unspoken code between them. Sidna Edwards or Claude Allen fired first. Dexter Goad fired second shot hitting Floyd Allen in his pelvis, who fell on his lawyer. Goad claimed he thought Allen was going for his gun. Floyd Allen started to unbutton his sweater, claiming later he was going for legal papers, while others thought he was going for a gun.

Sidna Allen fired the third shot at Goad and hit Judge Massie. Claude Allen shot Sheriff Webb, who he thought was trying to kill Floyd. Deputies began shooting at Floyd Allen.

Attorney David Bolen yelled at Floyd, "get off of me for God's sake before they kill me shooting at you." Deputy Clerk Woodson C. Quesenberry shot Floyd Allen with his .25 automatic, which he claimed he bought just to kill Floyd Allen. He hit Floyd in the right leg as he laid on the ground. A single, 25-year-old man at the time of the shootout, Quesenberry resigned after the event.

Floyd Allen pulled his own weapon and began to return fire. Floyd emptied his weapon in the courtroom. Wesley Edwards came forward shooting at Sheriff Webb, emptied his .32 caliber automatic before leaving the room. His brother, Sidna Edwards ran to the railing, but never fired a shot as his mother, Alberta, grabbed his arm and stopped him before he ruined his life too. Floyd grabbed Sidna Edward's pistol and ran into the streets of Hillsville, where he continued to shoot at jurors as they ran down the street.

Friel Allen shot Commonwealth Attorney Foster, killing him. He stumbled into the Jury Room and fell over dead on the woodpile with a law book in one hand and a gun in the other very symbolic of the day's events.

Claude Allen shot at Goad and Webb, killing juror Augustus Fowler, who was hit in the right side of the head as he got up to run. Fowler was moved to the Thornton Hotel, where he died on Saturday at 1 p.m. Victor Allen, luckily for him, had no gun with him that day.

Sidna Allen reloaded at least once and continued to shoot at Goad. Sidna was the last Allen to leave the room. Goad had two pistols a .38 and .32 caliber. He grabbed a pistol from Peter Easter and shot Sidna Allen in the left arm as he went down the courthouse steps. Goad continued his pursuit of the Allens. He shot Floyd in the right knee, who returned fire, which might be the bullet holes in steps number 8 and 13 of the courthouse. The shootout at the courthouse was over.

Bullets and spectators went out the windows of the courtroom. There were more windows then than today. In a humorous aside, Ron Hall, who wrote the best book on this subject tells the story of his relative, Gurtis Hall, who went out the window and promptly ran into an apple tree, dislocating his shoulder. When asked if he ran, Hall said, "No, but I passed a lot of people who were."

"A sense of self-preservation suddenly and forcefully presented itself." Sidna Allen wrote later that it was like a "bad dream," where you had "better act or be killed." "Guns flashed and roared...men cried out in fright, Women screamed, and the wounded moaned in agony." Overturned tables, chairs, and benches became protection

It lasted about ninety seconds with fifty-seven shots, others believe over sixty, being fired. When it was over Sheriff Lewis Webb, Judge Thornton Massie, Commonwealth Attorney William Foster, and Juror Augustus C. Fowler were all dead. A young woman named Nancy Elizabeth Ayers would be dead by the end of the next day. While there might be many circumstances that caused the massacre in the courtroom, the fact is that six people died, and seven received wounds. The shootout produced five widows and thirty-two fatherless children.

Dexter Goad had one wound, which went through his cheek, chipped a tooth, went out his neck, and took off his collar button. Goad sent a telegraph to Governor Mann saying, "Send troops to the county of Carroll at once. Mob violence…" Dexter Goad became a lawyer and lived until 1939.

Deputy Elihu Gillespie had one wound. He hid behind a turned over bench and lost a fingertip when he exposed it. Christopher Columbus Cain was shot twice in his back and right leg, the latter came out seventeen years. Andrew Howlett was shot once in the back while protecting his family, his wife, and son. Stuart Worrell shot in his backside.

Sheriff Lew Webb had five wounds, two in the back and three in his front. He fell backward and shot into the ceiling dying instantly. His toothpick was still in his mouth when they found him.

William Foster was shot six times including the stomach, head, and arm. Judge Massie was shot three times and drowned in his own blood. He lived for fifteen minutes and told anyone who would listen that "Sid Allen shot me."

Witness Nancy Elizabeth "Betty" Ayers, age 17, was shot in the back. She had witnessed the fight between Floyd Allen and Deputy Samuels. She went home and died the next day.

Most of the Allens went down "Jail Alley" and got on horses to make their escape, but Floyd Allen could not make it due to his three wounds. Floyd tried to mount a horse but fell off in agony over his shattered femur bone. He stayed in the Blankenship Feed Stable for an hour. Victor Allen stayed with his father, Floyd, standing over him to protect him in what one author described as "in disbelief." Floyd was moved to the Elliott House Hotel. The rest of the Allens met at Jack Allen's house except for Claude Allen and Sidna Edwards. They thought they could all "hide out" until things calmed down. They were nursing their wounds too. Sidna was shot once.

Miraculously all the deputies disappeared from Hillsville, leaving it lawless at the time it was most needed. No phones were working because the operator, Ella Wilcox was in the toilet. Vigilantes under the leadership of Ellis Worrell built bonfires.

Riders went to Guynn's store in Woodlawn and Baker's Station in Sylvatus. They called Governor William Hodges Mann. In 1912, there were no Virginia State Police, so he sent Baldwin Felts Detectives along with National Guardsmen.

Thomas Lafayette Felts was born in Carroll County. He was in Bluefield at the time of the shootings. He took the train to Galax with seven detectives. The next day on Friday he arrested Floyd, and Victor Allen along with any "bystanders" he felt were involved. Floyd, when he finally arrived in jail, tried to cut his throat.

William Baldwin, Felt's partner, was security for the Norfolk and Western Railroad and was prominent in the Hatfields and McCoys Feud along the nearby West Virginia and Kentucky border. The agency became infamous later for breaking up coal strikes. Described as a "rough, mean, ruthless crew," the Baldwin Felts Detectives offered a $3,500 reward "Dead or Alive" for the fugitive Allens and their family members involved. Carroll County residents remained amazingly quiet about the location of the missing Allens.

Later in life, Sidna Allen never divulged who hid them. Claude Allen and Sidna Edwards were alone and simply went home, but later surrendered. Sidna and Friel Allen along with Wesley Edwards were together. The three hid out at Caroline Allen Easter, Friel's sister's barn at night and the nearby woods during the day. Friel Allen's father negotiated a five-year sentence if he surrendered.

The weather that March was very cold, but Sidna Allen and Wesley Edwards hid out for a month before walking to Winston-Salem, North Carolina. They boarded a train that took them to Asheville and then on to Des Moines, Iowa, where they lived at Lucille Cameron's Boarding House, working as carpenters.

The sensationalism began at once about the shootout. Images of six of the perpetrators were sold on a one cent postcard. One of the images was of Byrd Marion, who was not indicted for the crime. Later convicted of moonshining, Marion died suspiciously of "pneumonia" in prison where every bone in his body was broken. The mothers and wives hid photos of the missing Sidna and Wesley Allen.

311

The New York Times's lead story on March 15 was about the shootout with sensational stories about riders bringing their horses into the courtroom. For two weeks, it was on the front page of the Roanoke Times, and most of it was "Fake News." The Bluefield Daily Telegraph wrote that "A troop of desperadoes rode down from the Blue Ridge Mountains to Carroll County Court House and opened fire on officials as the sentence was being passed upon Floyd Allen...Floyd drew himself up to his full height fired and killed Judge Massie."

Newspaper stories continued to sensationalize the story bringing out all the stereotypes of the South's violent culture. It was not until the Titanic sank on April 15, 1912, that Hillsville came off the front pages of the national papers. Some went so far as to call for the genocide of the rural people of southwest Virginia.

The Baltimore Evening Sun wrote on March 15, 1912, "There are but two remedies for such a situation as this, and they are education and extermination. With many of the individuals, the latter is the only remedy. Men and races alike, when they defy civilizations must die. The mountaineers of Virginia and Kentucky and North Carolina like the Red Indians and the South African Boers, must learn this lesson."

One man with the interesting name of Valentine Hatfield said, "We have been tried, convicted, and sentenced by the press before they knew the facts of our case." A reporter named Alexander Forward called it "the most horrible and dastardly blow at civilization in the history of Virginia."

In June 1912, Wesley returned to Carroll County to see his girlfriend, Maude Iroler. He gave her $50 to come to Des Moines and marry him. While the stories of what happened next are all over the place. Most believe that Maude's father turned in the lovebirds, and came with her and three detectives to capture the two fugitives on September 14, 1912, in return for $500 in reward money. In December, Maude married another man and did not admit her part in the capture until 1957.

The train brought Sidna Allen and Wesley Edwards back to Roanoke, Virginia. There were trials in Wytheville. Floyd and Claude Allen received death sentences. Sidna, tried six months later, received thirty-five years. Wesley Edwards got twenty-seven years. Sidna Edwards got eighteen years. He plead guilty to second-degree murder even though he did not shoot in the courtroom that day in March 1912. His mother feared a death penalty and got him to plead. Friel Allen got eighteen years instead of the five his father, Victor, negotiated with Baldwin Felts Detectives.

Virginia seized Floyd and Sidna Allen's property. There were wrongful death lawsuits. Judge Massie's estate got Floyd's land. The estates of Massie, Foster, and Webb received Sidna's land, which was estimated to be worth $40,000. Wives and children were evicted from their land. Bodies were buried within two days with no autopsies performed. Bullets became souvenirs and not evidence.

Floyd Allen and Claude were put to death via electricity on March 28, 1913. Floyd first at 1:22 p.m. with Claude following a few minutes later. Floyd received 2,000 volts with smoke coming from his wrists and took four minutes to die. Jack Allen picked up their bodies at the train station in Mount Airy, North Carolina.

Their funerals were at Floyd's house at the foot of the Blue Ridge, which still stands today and buried nearby. Floyd's tombstone stated, "Sacred to the memory of Claude. S Allen and his father, who was judicially murdered in the Virginia Penitentiary March 28, 1913, by order of the Governor of the State over the protest of 100,000 citizens of the state of Virginia." It was placed underneath the present grave marker as part of the deal to pardon Sidna Allen.

In 1923, Wesley and Sidna Edwards were pardoned and lived near Richmond. Friel came back to Carroll County after being pardoned but moved to California. Victor Allen moved to New Jersey.

Sidna Allen worked as the foreman of the woodworking shop in the state penitentiary in Richmond. In 1926, Governor Harry Byrd, a Democrat, pardoned Sidna, who moved to Eden, North Carolina. He later lived on Orchard Street in Mount Airy. He took his unusual furniture touring around in the 1930s selling his memoirs and furniture from his truck. The Carroll County

Historical Society has several examples of his work. He is buried in Eden after dying of prostate cancer in 1941 in Hillsville.

The shootout is tourism in Carroll County these days. In 2012, on the one-hundredth anniversary of the event, a play and a symposium studied many aspects of the tragedy. Frank Levering staged his play "Thunder in the Hills" in the actual courthouse. It and later plays raised money to restore the Sidna Allen House. There were deputies on hand for the performance of the play, "Just in case." Frank Levering said that the "heat" he felt growing up in Carroll County had subsided as the memories of one hundred years ago had as well.

Joey Haynes, who played Dexter Goad in the play said of the real-life people specifically the Allens I expect. "I think they thought what they did was extremely justifiable to them. They were bothered by people who had gone off to get an education coming back and feeling like they were better than the common people." I found this statement extremely timely in the Age of Trump when education or expertise invokes envy instead of congratulation. This is something I have felt with my work to preserve history and the reaction to Democratically controlled clique in Patrick County. This lack of intellectualism is a slippery slope that should be a cautious lesson from the history involving the shootout in Hillsville.

Ron Hall believes Floyd Allen would have won his freedom on appeal. He thinks Allen went to court that day in 1912 to intimidate and did not plan the shootout. The facts lead this author to believe that if Floyd Allen accepted the fact that he was outsmarted by the courthouse clique and took his punishment that no one would have died that day in Hillsville. It appears to have been an obvious set up that Floyd Allen fell for as they knew he would not accept his punishment.

Was it fair, absolutely not, but killing people is not fair either. The fact that the Allens were positioned all around the courtroom that day tends to make this author believe it was deliberate and they did plan something for that day. Everyone has an opinion on this. When I saw the play written by Frank Levering, I was so impressed by Attorney Tom Jackson's portrayal of Floyd Allen that I came to dislike him intensely, which was either good acting on Jackson's part or I was disgusted by Allen's behavior and what it led too, six dead people.

In 1974, the Sidna Allen House went on the National Register of Historic Places. In 2014, the Carroll County Historical Society took ownership of the Sidna Allen house from Skip and Bonnie Widener Wood, and Stanley Widener. In 2016, the house was jacked up on steel beams to stabilize the house and placed back on its new cinder block foundation. Wolfe House Movers of Pennsylvania lifted the house and placed it on "cribs," wooden support pieces. The seventy stained glass windows were removed to protect them. Anyone interested in supporting the efforts to restore the Sidna Allen House should contact the Carroll County Historical Society at P. O. Box 937, Hillsville, VA 24343 or www.carrollvamuseum.org.

Jack Allen, a farmer and sawmill operator, was once described as having the "courage of a lion" might have been the last victim of the shootout. "If let alone, he was quiet and peaceful citizen, but once aroused he would fight to the death." He fought to the death In March 1916 when it is believed that Will

McCraw at the behest of the Baldwin Felts Detectives shot him to death on his way back from Mount Airy at the home of Mrs. Roberta Martin. It was rumored his death was over the duplicity involved in Friel's surrender and the five-year sentence. McCraw was found not guilty after two hours of deliberation. He claimed Jack struck him and thought his life was in danger. Others thought the courthouse clique had struck again.

The shootout at the Hillsville Courthouse was the most infamous event to occur in Southwest Virginia, but out of it came one of the most positive people to ever live in the area. Jasper "Jack" Allen married Katie Easter and had twelve children including seven boys. One of the boys, Barnett Allen, was charged, but acquitted in connection to the shootout. Barnett Allen was born 21 years before the shootout and only lived until 1926.

Jack's son, Barnett, had a daughter, Herma, who married Raymond Beamer. Their son, Frank, played football at Hillsville High School before matriculating to Virginia Tech, where he wore #25 and went on to become the winningest football coach in the history of our alma mater. Frank Beamer said his mother never wanted to talk about the shootout. He wrote a paper and gave a speech about it in a speech course at Virginia Tech, where he got an A. Herma Allen Beamer lived with the stigma of being an Allen in Carroll County. She lost her father, Barnett, to pneumonia, and her house to a fire in a year around age seven. Herma grew up with great inner determination and stayed a Democrat in a mostly Republican county. She became a teacher, and today her son has a reader program called Herma's Readers that donates books to schools. Her son, Frank, suffered burns to his face from a fire about the same age and he too became determined in life. The residuals from the shootout changed the lives of later generations on both sides of the event. Bringing this story full circle, in December 2015, Frank Beamer donated $5,000 to the restoration of the Sidna Allen house. He said at the time, "The main thing I always knew is that there were two sides to the story...Certainly a bunch of people getting shot in the courthouse, that doesn't need to happen, regardless of your side of the story." Sadly, it was not the last time Frank Beamer had to deal with a shooting in Southwest Virginia.

The courtroom today is much larger than it was in 1912.

Photos of the preservation of the Sidna Allen home along Highway 52 in Carroll County, just south of Hillsville, Virginia.

The Carroll County Courthouse in Hillsville, Virginia.

Floyd Allen.

Photos courtesy of Doug Stegall

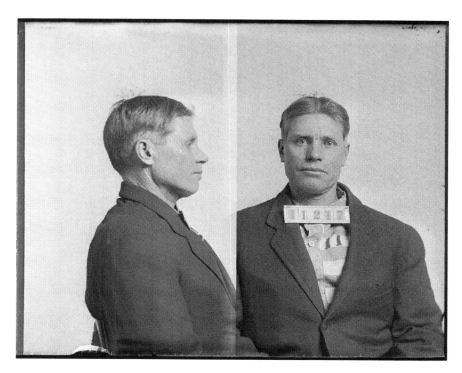

Above, Sidna Allen. Below, a record about the Hillsville Shootout.

Sidna Allen and Wesley Edwards after capture.

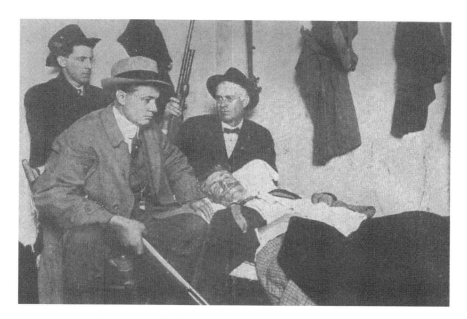

Above and below, Floyd Allen after capture.

Above, Baldwin-Felts detectives Payne and Lucas searching for the Allens at Bald Rock Knob. Below, a postcard with the Allens and others was sold after the shootout including Byrd Marion.

Dexter Goad.

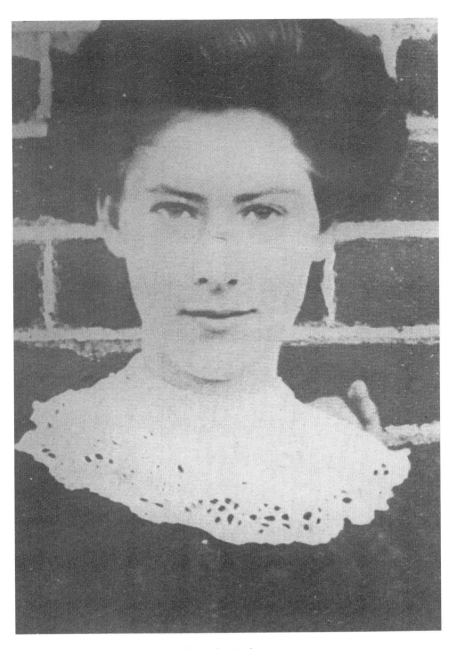

Maude Iroler.

Claude Allen.

Judge Thornton Massie.

Above, the home of Floyd Allen.

Below, the home of Sidna Allen at the time of the shootout.

Back row, Victor Allen, Byrd Marion and Sidna Edwards. Front row, Claude, and Friel Allen.

Above, posse headed out to search for the Allens.
Below, deputies sworn in the day after the shootout.

Above, Buzzard's Roost, one of the Allen hiding places. Below, a posse along the North Carolina state line searching for the Allens.

Above, moving Floyd to Roanoke. Below, Wray Horgan, Ernest Baldwin, and Harry Patton guarding the Wytheville Jail during one of the trials.

The path to Floyd Allen's moonshine still. Below, posse hunting for the Allens.

Today, the courthouse steps still have bullet holes in them.

Above, one of the bullet holes from the 1912 shootout. Below, the view today from those steps with the Confederate Monument.

Main Street in Hillsville, Virginia, near the time of the shootout.

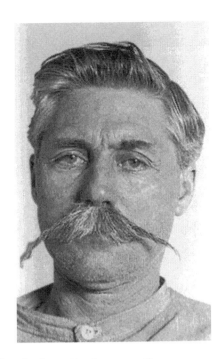

Above, Claude and Floyd Allen before their execution.
Below, the survivor, Sidna Allen while in prison.

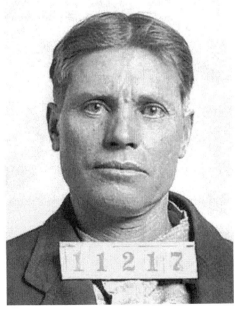

The graves of Floyd and Claude Allen.

Jasper "Jack" Allen, brother Floyd and Sidna Allen and ancestor of Frank Beamer.

Frank Beamer when he played football at Virginia Tech.

Burruss Hall at Virginia Tech

Chapter Fifteen:

<u>EMBRACING TRAGEDY AT VIRGINIA TECH</u>

On April 16, 2007, Frank Beamer entered a room with the victim's families. He said, "I had to walk to the front [of the room] ...and when I turned around and saw those eyes and the hurt and the pain and the suffering it just made an impression that I'll never forget. They sent their kids to college...and then all of a sudden it ends up it the saddest day of my life...You're telling them, 'We're never going to forget you and you're always going to be part of Virginia Tech,' but you just wish you could do more to take some of that load off their heart...I can honestly say I never saw so much pain in my life. Their faces will never disappear from my memory."

Beamer said he cried a long time that day, but his presence went a long way helping those people and all of us embrace the tragedy at Virginia Tech. He canceled spring football practice and the spring game, but it was football that later allowed us all to embrace the tragedy of that day.

That same day, April 16, 2007, I watched on television the horrible actions of one very sick individual at my alma mater in Blacksburg, Virginia. People, who I had not heard from in years, contacted me about it because of my known affection and support of Virginia Tech. The horror of that week was mixed with the pride of seeing Hokie students on national television showing their emotions, the courage that many of them showed facing a murderer, and the positive feelings toward their school. They were a credit to their parents and their university.

The disgust I have felt towards the events this week is as strong for the irresponsible media reporting of the events especially aimed at Virginia Tech President Charles Steger and the law enforcement officers. I was particularly incensed by the interview by UVA graduate Katie Couric, who went after Steger, showing her biased against the state's land-grant university. It was a bad week for Katie as one humorous moment came at the end of convocation when the "Wahoo" identified then Hokie Football Coach Frank Beamer as the President of the United States.

At the convocation, President Steger received a standing ovation and a long embrace from then Governor and later Vice-Presidential candidate, Tim Kaine. Kaine said that day, "...in the darkest moment in the history of this university, the world saw you and saw you respond in a way that built community."

It never sits well when someone attacks a member of your family, but when you are a member of the family, it is sometimes hard to look at their actions, but I decided that I must take a hard look at the events of that April day that so marked my alma mater. Mistakes were made, but in studying history, you can only judge someone by their actions based on what they knew at the time. Monday morning quarterbacking and blaming President Steger or the law enforcement officials for the act of a mentally ill individual is the easy way out especially for journalists. We do not know if they had locked down the university, an almost impossible action due to the size and number of people involved, that the killer would not have just found other victims. No one could predict these events or say what would have happened. What bothered me most after studying these events is the lack of simple common sense in what to me is an obvious lack of follow through before, during, and after these events.

When Nikki Giovanni ended the convocation with her "We Are Virginia Tech" remarks followed by cheering, seeing the students filling Lane Stadium and the vigil at the Drillfield later that night, I felt great pride in being part of a university that has such great students and their defiance in the face of overwhelming grief not to give up.

On the Drillfield in front of Burruss Hall, thirty-three stones appeared including one for the shooter. It was removed, replaced, and removed again. Today, there are only thirty-two stones for the victims of the shooter and not for him. His sister said, "He has made the world weep."

No one can begin to understand the feelings of those who lost children, siblings, and friends that week at Virginia Tech, but the outpouring of support for them is something I will never forget. That week, I read fans from West Virginia, the University of Virginia, Auburn, East Carolina, LSU, Texas A&M, UNC-Greensboro, and every university I could imagine on internet websites saying repeatedly "We Are All Hokies." I saw students at UNC-Asheville, Central Florida, Duke, N. C. State, and many others hold candlelight vigils. I thought that like the embrace from the Governor Kaine to President Steger that said it all. Everyone embraced Virginia Tech during the aftermath and I think everyone became Hokies that week to embrace the tragedy.

One week and one day after the tragic events of April 16, 2007, I returned to the campus of Virginia Tech to return some books to the Newman Library, a place I spend more time at now than I did when I was a student in Blacksburg in the early 1980s. I took my digital camera and my memories of twenty-six years ago when I first came to the campus driven through some horrible fog by Greg Radford, who was thinking of going to school there too. Virginia Tech founded in 1872 as Virginia's land-grant university began with many men who served under Patrick County's most famous son James Ewell Brown "Jeb" Stuart involved along with John Penn, who worked in the Virginia House of Delegates to start the school. Virginia Tech continues a strong military tradition with the Corps of Cadets, who sadly had one member fall victim on

April 16.

After parking and walking to the library, where I came upon

a memorial display about the victims and related books related to

their chosen fields of study, I headed out across campus. The first

place was the Memorial Chapel that notes those from Virginia

Tech who received the Medal of Honor in service to the United

States.

Seldom have I visited the chapel during my time as a

student or since, but on this day, I found many orange and

maroon items on top of the chapel that faces towards the

Drillfield and Burruss Hall in one direction and Torgerson Bridge

facing towards Blacksburg in the other direction. There were

people everywhere on campus that day, but it was strangely

quiet. I went inside the Chapel and found many items in honor of

those who passed and outside an opportunity to write a message

with the many hanging messages on strings tied across.

I walked up towards McBryde Hall, where I had most of my

classes including the largest Civil War class in the nation under

James I. "Bud" Robertson, who I believe would have been holding a class that morning with 300 students just two buildings away from Norris Hall, where most lost their lives. I went in and sat down in the auditorium where I spent so many enjoyable mornings with one of the best teachers I ever had.

I made my way outside again and moved towards Norris Hall, still surrounded with yellow crime tape, and guarded by a lone Virginia State Trooper as all sorts of criminal investigators and staff went past us both. I turned and walked into Patton Hall and found a memorial for those engineering students and facility in the lobby.

Outside again, I walked along the sidewalk and up to face Norris Hall and many flowers and notes remembering those who perished in the building. I looked at Burruss Hall, the administration building, where many people congregated around, but still, it was strangely silent in respect for those who died.

I crossed the street and made my way to the thirty-three "Hokie Stones" placed in a semi-circle around the observation point in front of the building. There were names for the thirty-two victims and one stone without a name, which I assumed was for the shooter. I walked around the stones looking at the flowers, gifts, and messages for these people. The silence was deafening except for the sound of busses from Blacksburg Transit. I watched people who were obviously just "long necking" as was I, but I saw students becoming emotional, and I thought, but for the grace of God go I. Trying to find logic and reason in something so horrific is impossible.

I walked back towards the library through the Drillfield past trees tied in orange and maroon ribbons. A Baptist group gave me bottled water. I stopped and drank in the cold water and the scene as I looked back towards the scene of the tragedy and the memorial. I thought about Ryan Clark, the member of the Marching Virginians from my mother's hometown of Augusta, Georgia, who lost his life going to the defense of the first victim Emily Hilscher in West Ambler Johnson Hall. I thought about Liviu Librescu, who survived the madness of Adolph Hitler to lose his life defending his students against the madness of a student.

Mostly, I thought about the loss of such a great group of people and the pride I felt in the university I graduated.

I wandered up to Squires Student Center to find many people watching a press conference from law enforcement about the events, but what overwhelmed me were the banners from all over the country from other universities signed by thousands of students. I did not know there was a University of Mobile, but I knew that this tragic event had made them all Hokies. Thomas Wolfe wrote "You Can't Go Home Again," but You Can Go Hokie Again.

Major League Baseball showed support as the Washington Nationals of the National League wore Virginia Tech hats. The DC United soccer team wore Virginia Tech jerseys.

The Yankees invaded Virginia Tech. Not the Yankee soldiers of General George Crook in 1864, when he visited the Preston and Olin Institute, eight years before it became Virginia Agricultural and Mechanical College due to the 1862 Morrill Land Grant College Act. The university was literally born during the Civil War. It was not the Yankee cavalry of George Stoneman's cavalry, who visited in April 1865, but the New York Yankees, the storied

Major League Baseball team. The exhibition game played at

English Field that day continued the yearlong trend of those many

supporting Virginia Tech after the tragedy of April 16, 2007.

"On May 23, 2007, prior to their game against the Boston

Red Sox on that day, the Yankees made a $1 million contribution

to the Hokie Spirit Memorial Fund and announced that they

would visit the Hokies to aid in the healing process. Derek Jeter

jogged onto the field to present the check just minutes before the

Yankees took the field against the Red Sox in the final game of a

three-game series." George Steinbrenner, the owner of the

Yankees, said, "The events that took place this spring in Virginia

have deeply affected us all," Steinbrenner said in a statement.

"...the Virginia Tech community has shown great spirit and resolve

during this challenging time, and the New York Yankees are proud

to join so many others in supporting the healing process."

Charles Steger said after meeting Steinbrenner, "I could

also tell from the tone of his voice and what he said that he's

sincere and committed, and really feels it's important to take this kind of step to help these young people regain their lives."

According to Steger, the Yankees are the only sports team to contribute money to Virginia Tech.

Running out to their positions, the Yankees' starting lineup passed the Virginia Tech logos painted near the first and third base dugouts. Jorge Posada caught Steger's pitch in front of a nationally televised audience, a throw that came in low but reachable. The catcher said that it is an honor for him to wear the Virginia Tech logo on his cap — as the entire team did on Wednesday — and that he is proud of the way the organization stood behind those at the school. "The things that went on at Virginia Tech … it just puts things in perspective," Posada said. "Baseball is not everything, and you [take] your life for granted. But this is an example of the great organization we are representing. I think the Yankees are doing the right thing." So, even the "Damn" Yankees embraced the tragedy at Virginia Tech.

Closer to home Virginia Governor Tim Kaine appointed a Review Panel on April 19, 2007, at the cost of $750,000 to review and report back to him. The Chairman of the group was Colonel

Gerald Massengill, a retired Virginia State Policeman. Vice-Chairman was Dr. Marcus Martin, Professor of Emergency Medicine at the University of Virginia. Other members included Gordon Davies, former Director of the State Council of Higher Education, Dr. Roger Depue, formerly of the FBI, Carroll Ellis, Director of Fairfax County Police Department's Victim Services Division, Tom Ridge, former Governor of Pennsylvania and Secretary of Homeland Security, Dr. Aradhana Sood, Professor of Psychiatry and Pediatrics at Virginia Commonwealth University and Diane Strickland, former Judge of the 23rd Judicial Circuit Court. No members of the families or those representing them made it onto the panel.

In the aftermath, Governor Kaine refused to remove President Steger or Police Chief Flinchum. The panel concluded on August 30, 2007, with seventy preventive recommendations. The report itself had several omissions that led to sharp criticism and changes specifically about the timeline when President Steger knew about events on that day in April 2007. Collusion and thoughts of CYA "Cover Your Ass" came to mind in reading about the report. Finally, in December 2009, the panel released the final report.

What this report discovered were the multiple omissions that allowed Cho's mental health to fall through the cracks due to the wrong interpretation of the privacy laws. The Family Education and Rights Privacy Act "allows schools to disclose those records without the consent of the following parties or under the following condition. School officials with legitimate educational interest." This was not done in Cho's case and led to the right hand at Virginia Tech not knowing what the left hand was dealing with this troubled young man.

Virginia Tech dropped the ball by allowing so much time to elapse between the first two shootings and the massacre in Norris Hall. The Virginia Tech Emergency Response Plan states at a Level III incident is "an incident occurring at the university that adversely impacts or threatens life, health or property at the university on a large scale." Virginia Tech should have locked down after the first two shootings. That is just common sense. We do not know if it would have saved thirty lives in Norris Hall, but it was the right thing to do, and the university failed at the crucial moment. The Clery Act states that "institutions must provide timely warnings in a manner likely to reach all members of the campus." Virginia Tech sent out warnings for mundane actions such as mold in the library, measles and mumps outbreaks, multiple bomb threats, the previously mentioned Morva incident, but not when two students were found gunned down in their dorm. Where was the common sense and the concern for the safety of the innocents on campus?

In March 2011, the Department of Education fined Virginia Tech $55,000 for waiting too long to notify the campus, which overturned and then reinstated by the Secretary of Education in September 2012.

Retired Virginia State Police Colonel Gerald Massengill, who later served on Governor Kaine's panel on the Virginia Tech shootings said it plainly, "Mental health is the big issue that came out of Virginia Tech." Colleges should have "Assessment Teams" that have law enforcement, mental health practitioners, administrators, and academics.

Today, students must agree to counseling to stay a student at Virginia Tech. Appointments are tracked, and progress is noted. The requirements to commit someone over mental health issues have been eased. James Reinhard, Medical Director of the Cook Counseling Center that was involved, was not optimistic about the changes stating, "limited amount of money, spends all its time chasing its tail with a crisis...we still don't get it. That's not going to fix the system."

Massengill does not believe that a campus shutdown would have been possible in 2007, while today it is commonplace. He does believe that a campus flooded with police might have caught the shooter before he got to Norris Hall that day. He believes the Kaine report was too quick and not all the voices were heard. It was a mental health issue and not a gun issue. The police assumed a single theory relating to the possibility of a domestic issue and ignored the idea of a mass shooting on campus that day.

In January 2008, President George W. Bush signed HR 2640, the National Instant Criminal Background Check legislation

(NICBCS), the first gun control legislation since 1994, which closed loopholes that allowed people who had been "adjudicated" and were mentally unsound to purchase handguns. In 2008, the Family Education Rights and Privacy Act (FERPA) changed the regulations regarding education records for the U. S. Department of Education.

After the shootings, Virginia distributed 35 million to mental health in the Commonwealth, but in the six years that followed the legislature cut mental health by 4.5 million. Richard Bonnie, a UVA law professor, and chairman of the Chief Justice Commission on Mental Health in Virginia from 2006-11 stated," "Unfortunately, nothing got put in place. Well, then you have another tragedy." It was felt by many that the focus was put on hospital bed rather than community services that would keep people from needing them. Funding for the patients with no private insurance or Medicaid is also an issue. In 2013, Virginia ranked #35 of 50 in funding behavioral health with half of that going to state hospitals.

Thirty-two separate endowment funds were set up with 3.2 million dollars, which had grown to over 7 million by the end of 2007. In 2008, Virginia Tech paid eleven million dollars to twenty-eight families, and surviving victims received anywhere from $11,000 to 208,000.

Two families filed separate actions, and two families did not sue at all. Virginia Tech paid the medical expenses for the injured. The two families of Erin N. Petersen and Julia K. Pryde took Virginia Tech to civil court. In March 2012, a jury found the university guilty of negligence in not warning the campus. Civil trials have a lower standard of proof than a criminal trial. The case of O. J. Simpson comes to mind in discussing this when the Goldman and Brown families won in civil court, while a criminal jury found Simpson not guilty. The jury awarded the families of Pryde and Petersen 4 million dollars, reduced to $100,000 as Virginia law allows. The Virginia Supreme Court in what many viewed as a very political decision invoked "common sense" to reverse the verdict.

In 2007, the second floor of Norris Hall became a Center for Peace and Violence Prevention. Across the street in front of Burruss Hall, there are thirty-two "Hokie Stones" placed in a semicircle with the names of the victims and two benches honoring the survivors. The Special Collections Department of the Carol M. Newman Library holds 90,000 "tokens" of support from eighty different countries in 517 boxes that take up more than 500 cubic feet of space.

On September 1, 2007, Virginia Tech opened its football season with a game against East Carolina University. The ECU Athletic Director and former University of Virginia basketball coach Terry Holland presented a check for $100,000. As 32 orange balloons floated to the sky, the Hokies took the field to one of the loudest cheers ever heard in Lane Stadium.

Frank Beamer said of that day. "A football game, everybody's going in the same direction. Everybody wants to the very same thing...and I like being part of that...We all needed that...We weren't going to let this one sick individual define who

Virginia Tech was...I think we're going to be remembered by how we responded."

In 2017, ten years later I returned to Virginia Tech to view the campus a decade after the worst event in its history occurred. President George W. Bush sent a message stating, "A decade later, the pain is still fresh." Virginia Tech is not the worst shooting in American history now. Orlando with 49 deaths holds that dubious claim to fame. There were fifty Hokies who were killed or wounded that April day in 2007 including the shooter. He has become like Lord Voldemort in Harry Potter, "He who cannot be named."

Easter Sunday, April 16, 2017, dawned with the message of "new hope, new life." I walked around campus observing the people and activities remembering the saddest day in our university's history. What I remember most was the silence, silence of a Sunday morning, and silent respect for those who were gone and those who survived.

I went into the 7/11 for a Big Gulp full of Coke that usually had Wild Turkey in it on Saturdays when I was at Hokie football games. I walked down Main Street Blacksburg through a sea of Hokie Bird statues by the post office where the shooter mailed his manifesto to NBC. I walked near West Ambler Johnston and Norris Hall, where I saw a young lady sitting by herself, sobbing. I saw lots of Hokies United T-shirts that were brought back after many years of being unavailable. I saw Cindy Farmer of Fox8 in North Carolina, who was an alum and was doing live stories from Virginia Tech that weekend.

On Sunday, I saw Virginia Governor Terry McAuliffe, who as usual turned the event into a plea for gun control and Virginia Tech's new President Sands, who was just a little too politically correct for me that day. The one person who I thought was real that weekend was Tim Kaine, who was Governor when the shootings occurred. Just a few months from losing to Donald Trump and Mike Pence as Hillary Clinton's Vice-Presidential candidate in what I thought was just a way to secure Virginia for the Democrats, Kaine was obviously emotional in his remarks ten years later as he was in 2007.

The survivors are still Hokies. Dereck O'Dell, who was 19 in 2007 from Roanoke County was shot in his right arm and found other bullet holes in his black fleece jacket later. He is now a Veterinarian, married with a daughter. He was in 207 Norris Hall that day and helped bar the door with other classmates.

Kevin Sterne was shot twice and nearly died underwent years of physical therapy on his legs. He is in the famous photo while being carried by four police by Alan Kim of the Roanoke Times. He still works at Virginia Tech, the only victim who still does. He is 32 now with BS and MS degrees in Electrical Engineering and has a son.

Former President George W. Bush sent a message on the tenth anniversary said it best that we wrote, "Don't be overcome evil, but overcome evil with good." Kaine else said that day that we do not have to be heroes, but we should stop being bystanders.

Could Virginia Tech's campus have been locked down? On December 8, 2011, Ross Ashely murdered Virginia Tech Police Officer Derek Crouse. The campus at once went into lockdown. I know this because I was in the library that day doing research on the myriad of book projects I work on. I felt no annoyance at having my freedom curtailed that day as I know at what cost we must endure to protect ourselves.

I refrained from showing photos of the victims at Virginia Tech in this chapter as their families are still very much alive unlike many of the chapters in this book. I encourage the reader to visit this website and take the time to get to know these thirty-two amazing human beings who lost their lives much too soon.

Norris Hall, where most of the killings occurred at Virginia Tech is beside Burruss Hall, where the President's office resides.

Above, Norris Hall. Below, the U. S. Post Office in Blacksburg,
where Cho mailed his manifesto to NBC News.

The memorial to the victims and survivors is located in front of Burruss Hall at Virginia Tech.

Above, West Ambler Johnston Hall, where first two killings occurred. Below, Harper Hall, where the killer lived before the shootings.

Above, one of the thirty-two Hokie stones honoring the victims.
Below, the circular memorial with stones for the victims.

Above, Burruss Hall. Below, the memorial to the victims and survivors in front of the same building.

Hokie Stones honoring the first two victims. Below, McBryde Hall, where the largest Civil War class in the country occurred that same morning just yards away from the worst school shooting in the U. S. history up to that time.

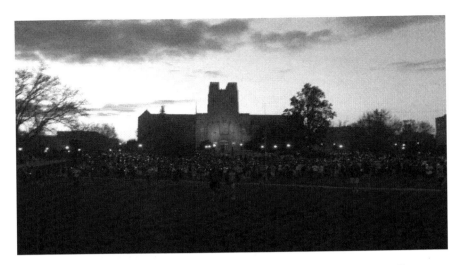

The candlelit vigil in April 2017 in front of Burruss Hall.

The author with Virginia Tech alumni Cindy Farmer of FOX8 in North Carolina at the April 2017 remembrance of the shootings at Virginia Tech. Below, at the statue of William Addison Caldwell, the first student at Virginia Tech.

https://www.weremember.vt.edu/

Afterword:

<u>CURTAINS</u>

"So, when they continued asking him, he lifted up himself, and said unto them, He that is without sin among you, let him first cast a stone at her." John 8:7

Agatha Christie is the bestselling author of all time and what does she write about? Murder, whether it is Miss Marble or my favorite Hercule Poirot. I particularly like the David Suchet versions often seen on public television.

Two episodes come to mind when thinking about the dilemma that many of the people in this book dealt with. In *Murder On The Orient Express,* where our detective concludes that twelve people among the lovely Jessica Chastain inflicted twelve stab wounds on the victim, Mr. Ratchett, played by Toby Jones.

Poirot lectures the killers about "Vigilante Justice" and "Kangaroo Justice" and that they have no right to take the law into their own hands. "We become savages," he tells them when we become jury and executioner. "The Rule of Law must be held high and if it falls you pick it up and hold it higher." He continues his impassioned lecture telling them that society and civilized people will have nothing to shelter themselves if the rule of law is destroyed. They should let God administer higher justice. He tells those that are without sin to throw the first stone and God, not them, has the right to judge. Jesus did not throw the first stone at Stephen in the New Testament. Jesus turned the other cheek and forgave, but every page of this book is about people who whether out of rage, frustration or just took it upon themselves to be judge, jury, and executioner.

Even the great Hercule Poirot was guilty of murder. In the final episode of the long-running series titled *Curtains*, he kills. "I have no more to say. Am I justified in what I have done? I do not believe that a man should take the law into his own hands, but by taking a life, have I not saved others. I have always been so sure, but now when the moment comes I will not try to save myself, but humbly offer my soul to God and pray for his mercy. It is for him to decide." And then the great detective dies.

In the book, Poirot sends his longtime friend and crime solver Captain Hastings a message where he says the following. "Everyone is a potential murderer. In everyone there arises from time to time the wish to kill—though no the will to kill…I, who value human life—have ended my career by committing murder. Perhaps it is because I have been too self-righteous, too conscious of rectitude, that this terrible dilemma had to come to me. For you see, Hastings, there are two sides to it."

I am sure that many of my readers have at one time, or another thought about taking another's life at a moment of rage, but to throw your life away over someone who is not worthy is a mistake. Revenge in the form of success or outsmarting your potential victim is always sweeter. I have found that an amazing thing called "karma" manages to take care of things. I believe in God's Mercy for the victim and the killer.

I based these chapters on true stories as the movies say about real people, who made choices in the heat of the moment and sometimes planned. These are stories of sick minds and angry men who react before they think, but they all should remember what the "Good Book" says that you should not murder because the law speaks of justified killing when the perpetrators violate the law, man's and God's there are consequences for those who take another life. "You shall not murder."

So, ends my investigation into true crimes of the past. Looking at murder in a rearview mirror has been a fascination for me since as a boy my father would watch film noir movies and look over at me and say, "There is a killer in there somewhere."

In 2013, the History Channel broadcasted a show about the Hatfields and McCoys coming together to make moonshine together. *Hatfields and McCoys White Lightning* capitalized on their violent past against each other and combining it with alcohol reflects the way the feud between the two families is viewed by the American public at large, but the violence between them was a serious and deadly event in the late 1800s. I like to say that all things go back to the Civil War in the history of modern America whether it is States' Rights or Civil Rights and so it is for the feud between the Hatfields and the McCoys.

Randall McCoy played by Bill Paxton visited Anderson "Devil Anse" Hatfield played by Kevin Costner in the recent mini-series on the History Channel to ask for the return of his sons to take them back to Kentucky to face justice for the murder of Ellison Hatfield. McCoy damns Hatfield and Kevin Costner in what I can only describe as the essence of the feud, the bad feelings between these two men. Hatfield tells McCoy to bring up God one more time, and he will not make it home. "That might be Randall, but I don't recall God saving you that day. We saved each other because that is what men do in war. This is all here. This all sits the way it sits because of us and nobody else, but you feel the need to bring up God one more time, whose side he sits on, you won't be making the ride home."

Rather than meet his maker, McCoy choosing discretion as the better part of valor returns to Kentucky without his sons. Hatfield killed the McCoy boys in an act of vigilante justice unheard of today in these United States.

But, that is the story for another day or another book looking back at true crime and murder in the prism of the past, looking at it through a rear view mirror.

Selected Bibliography

"A Bomb for the Bridegroom" File, Mount Airy Museum of Regional History.

Bassett Historical Center Files
    Fayerdale
    Fayette Street Shootout
    Martinsville Seven

NEWSPAPERS
Eastern Shore News: April 20, 1994
Mount Airy Times: January 4, 1952;
Mount Airy News: December 2, 1920; October 7, 1936; October 8, 1936; October 10, 1936; October 15, 1936; October 16, 1936; January 24, 1993; July 6, 1994; December 14, 1997; December 21, 1997;
Richmond Times-Dispatch: February 6, 2011;
Winston-Salem Journal: January 6, 1952; April 8, 1954;

BOOKS AND MAGAZINES
Allen, Sidna. *Memoirs of J. Sidna Allen*. Leakesville, NC: 1929.
Beamer, Frank with Jeff Snook. *Let Me Be Frank: My Life at Virginia Tech*. Chicago, IL: 2013
Berrier, Ralph. *The Courthouse Tragedy: Gunfight in Hillsville in 1912*. Roanoke Times, March 10, 2012.
Berrier, Ralph. "Beamer Donates $5,000 to Allen House Restoration." Roanoke Times, December 11,2015.
Cariens, David S. *Virginia Tech: Make Sure It Doesn't Get Out*. Kilmarnock VA, 2014.
Cheek, April C. "The Hillsville Tragedy: Appalachian Stereotypes as Examined Through the Carroll County Courtroom Shootout of 1912." MA History Thesis, Virginia Tech, 1998.
Cooley, E. J. *The Inside Story of the World Famous Courtroom Tragedy*. Charlottesville, VA: 1915.
Hall, Ronald W. *The Carroll County Courthouse Tragedy*. Hillsville, VA: 1998
Hall, Ronald W. *A Hundred Years of Life and Crime in Old Carroll*. Hillsville, VA: 2013.
Haynes, Elmer. The Fayerdale Tragedy: Fairy Stone Park.

Jackson, Joe, and Burke, William F. Jr. *Dead Run: The Shocking Story of Dennis Stockton and Life on Death Row in America.* New York, 2000.

Jessup, J. Willis. *The Enigma of the Knitting Mill.* Inside Detective, February 1937, Vol. 4 No. 2

Lazenby, Ronald. Roanoker Magazine, May 2010.

Rise, Eric W. *The Martinsville Seven: Race, Rape, and Capital Punishment.* Charlottesville, VA: 1995.

Index

A

Adam, 180, 188, 197, 214
Adams, 188, 195
Adkins, 197, 221
Allen, 16, 17, 247, 261, 288, 290, 291, 292, 293, 294, 295, 296, 297, 299, 300, 302, 303, 304, 305, 306, 307, 308, 309, 310, 311, 312, 313, 314, 315, 316, 317, 318, 319, 320, 322, 324, 325, 326, 327, 331, 333, 334, 336, 338, 342, 343, 344, 385
Allen, Floyd, 295, 296, 300, 302, 304, 305, 317
Allen, Jack, 303, 309, 314
Allen, Sidna, 293, 306, 315, 318, 344, 385
Almond, 120, 122, 125
Andes, 55
Ankenman, 41
Ararat, 9, 15, 65, 147, 148, 149, 150, 151, 187, 190, 191, 192, 193, 198, 204, 206, 235, 382, 396
Armstrong, 192
Arnder, 236, 237, 238, 239, 240, 241, 242, 243, 248, 249, 250, 251
Arthur, 155, 158, 161, 162, 164, 165, 166, 167, 168, 169, 170, 214, 218, 273, 278
Athol, 110, 142
Augusta County, 191
Ayer, 210

B

Baldwin, 59, 112, 310, 314, 319, 328, 337
Baldwin Felts, 310, 314, 319
Banner, 78, 80, 81, 82, 175
Barlow, 259
Barnes, 103, 104
Barrow, 48, 101, 103, 104, 105
Battle, 111, 123, 124, 125, 126, 127, 144, 187, 203
Battle of Camden, 203
Beamer, 319, 320, 321, 344, 345, 347, 348, 364, 385
Bell, 192
Berrier, 179, 385
Berry Hill, 190
Bibey, 168
Bishop, 37
Bivens, 261
Blacksburg, 19, 31, 33, 35, 39, 277, 348, 351, 352, 354, 365, 370
Blankenship, 298, 299, 309
Bleakley, 80
Bolen, 301, 302, 305
Boone, 177, 178, 181
Bowman, 151, 241, 243, 244, 247, 249
Bowsman, 54
Boyd, 197, 202
Bradshaw, 181
Britt, 177
Broaddus, 110
Brook Cove, 155, 156
Browder Cemetery, 166, 169

Brown, 51, 65, 126, 166, 205, 352, 363
Bryant, 48
Buckingham County, 278
Buford, 195
Burks, 197
Burrows, 159
Burruss, 31, 39, 350, 352, 353, 363, 369, 371, 374, 376
Burton, 109
Bush, 41, 361, 365, 367
Bynum, 165
Byrd, 125, 311, 315, 328, 334
Byrd Marion, 311, 328, 334
Byrum, 180

C

Cain, 308
California, 149, 169, 315
Cameron, 311
Cape Charles, 75, 76, 77, 78, 81
Carlin, 191, 192, 202
Carney, 37
Carroll County, 15, 16, 53, 289, 290, 291, 292, 294, 295, 297, 299, 300, 304, 310, 312, 313, 315, 316, 318, 320, 322, 323, 385
Carter, 109, 115, 201
Cassell, 13
Chambers, 273
Chaney, 217, 218, 219, 220, 233
Charleston, South Carolina, 195
Chastain, 379
Check, 258, 259, 269, 361
Cheng, 38
Childress, 148, 189, 291
Cho, 19, 20, 21, 22, 23, 24, 25, 26, 27, 28, 29, 30, 34, 35, 36,

37, 38, 39, 40, 41, 42, 359, 370
Christie, Agatha, 379
Civil War, 2, 397
Clark, 30, 32, 354
Claudville, 235
Clay, 188
Clinton, 196
Cloud, 192
Cochrane, 174, 175, 176, 177, 178, 179, 181, 182, 184
Colman, 36
Columbine, 20, 35
Cook, 23, 25, 147, 148, 150, 360
Cornwallis, 187, 196, 203
Corps of Cadets, 38, 352
Couture-Novak, 38
Cox,, 211, 212, 214, 216, 219, 220
Craig County, 279
Cranwell, 277
CRC, 97, 117, 124, 127, 128
Creasy, 79
Crockett, 200
Crouse, 367
CSS Virginia, 209
Cubine, 109
Culler, 149

D

Dan River, 235, 236, 239, 240, 249, 250
Danville, 190
Danville and Western Railroad, 47, 98, 100
Darlington, 48
Davidson, 188, 189
Davies, 358

Dawson, 192, 193
Deadmon Center, 280
Delaware, 191
Democrats, 289, 290, 296, 366
Depue, 358
Dexter Goad, 295, 304, 308
Dial, 180
Dickerson, 54, 75, 79
Dickinson, 51
Dodson, 215, 228
Draughn, 178
DuBois, 117
Dyer, 51

E

Ealey, 116
Earing, 80
Edwards, 178, 180, 293, 294,
    296, 297, 298, 303, 304, 305,
    309, 311, 313, 315, 326, 334
Ellis, 215, 228, 309, 358
Epperly, 272, 273, 274, 275,
    276, 277, 278, 279, 280, 283,
    284
Ewell, 205
Ex Parte Virginia, 65, 69

F

Fairy Stone, 209, 210, 211, 216,
    222, 224, 232
Fancy Gap, 288, 296, 297, 299,
    301
Farmer, 366, 377
Fayerdale, 9, 209, 210, 211,
    214, 215, 217, 222, 224, 225,
    231, 232, 233
Fayette Street, 9, 47, 48, 58, 59,
    60, 112
Finney, 101, 102, 103

Fishburn, 222
Flinchum, 31, 32, 33, 358
Ford, 203
Forsyth County, 74, 197
Fort Chiswell, 200
Foster, 294, 295, 296, 301, 303,
    305, 307, 308, 314
Fox, 195
Franklin Street, 9, 175, 179,
    183, 184
Fugate, 222

G

Galax, 77, 80, 310
Gates, 203, 241, 242
Georgia, 37, 95, 130, 354
Germanton, 155, 156, 157, 160,
    162
Gidens, 197, 202
Gilmer, 100
Gina Hall, 9, 273, 274, 275,
    276, 277, 278, 280, 285, 287
Giorno, 244, 246
Giovanni, 23, 350
Glock, 26, 42
Goad, 295, 299, 303, 304, 306,
    307, 316, 329
Goble, 253, 259, 265
Goblintown, 209, 222
Grace Moravian, 82, 91
Graham Mansion, 2
Granata, 41
Grayson, 63, 100, 101, 104,
    106, 107, 109, 113, 114, 121,
    124, 128, 129, 134, 291
Greene, 187, 197, 203
Gregory, 14, 51, 245, 246, 247
Griffith, Andy, 2, 74, 82, 175,
    182

Guilford Court House, 203
Guynn, 150, 310
Gwyn, 253, 254, 255, 261

H

Hairston, 56, 97, 100, 101, 102,
    103, 104, 105, 106, 107, 109,
    113, 115, 124, 128, 129, 135,
    136, 137, 190, 209
Hall, 28, 30, 31, 34, 35, 36, 39,
    41, 42, 43, 108, 198, 200,
    210, 211, 216, 217, 218, 219,
    220, 225, 229, 272, 274, 275,
    276, 277, 279, 280, 302, 306,
    317, 350, 352, 353, 354, 359,
    361, 363, 366, 367, 369, 370,
    371, 372, 374, 375, 376, 385
Hall, William, 198
Hampton, 27, 101, 103, 105,
    106, 109, 112, 114, 115, 124,
    128, 132, 164, 167, 210
Harass, 277
Hardin, 189
Harper Hall, 34, 372
Hatfields and McCoys, 53, 310,
    382
Hawks, 253, 254, 255, 259, 260,
    265
Haymore, 82
Haynes, 211, 212, 213, 216,
    217, 220, 296, 316
Hazel Hollow, 276, 280, 286
Heath, 161, 162, 163, 164
Hege, 72, 74, 75, 78, 79, 80, 81,
    82, 91
Help Save The Next Girl, 281
Helsabeck, 165
Henry, 397, 398

Henry County, 2, 8, 12, 47, 48,
    58, 60, 63, 97, 98, 105, 108,
    109, 111, 189, 191, 192, 193,
    194, 201, 213, 397, 398
Henry, Patrick, 57, 97, 192, 398

Herbert, 55, 293
Hill, 4, 11, 33, 37, 47, 48, 116,
    187, 192, 193, 194, 210, 256,
    294, 396
Hillsville, 9, 15, 54, 74, 75, 77,
    289, 290, 297, 298, 301, 304,
    305, 309, 312, 316, 317, 318,
    319, 322, 323, 325, 341, 385
Hilscher, 29, 30, 32, 34, 354
Hofer, 37
Holder, 257, 258, 259, 260, 261,
    271
Holley, 221
Hoskins, 179, 180
Hough, 32
Houston, 188, 189
Hundley, 56
Hunter's Chapel, 146, 148, 150
Hutcheson, 80

I

Iroler, 293, 313, 330

J

Jackson, 23, 73, 237, 274, 298,
    317, 385, 397
Jefferson, 195, 201
Jessup, 178, 181, 253, 254, 255,
    256, 259, 270, 385
Johnston, 23, 29, 43, 366, 372
Joyce, 109, 110, 245

K

Kaine, 349, 351, 357, 358, 360, 361, 366, 367
Kearfott, 109
Kibler Valley, 9, 234, 235, 236, 239, 241, 250
King's Mountain, 203
Knights of Pythias, 112
Kroll, 197

L

La Porte, 38
Lafferty, 210
Lanier, 55
Lankford, 80
Laurel Hill, 395, 396
Lawrence, 256, 257, 258, 268
Lawson, 9, 154, 155, 156, 158, 161, 162, 164, 165, 166, 167, 168, 169, 170, 171, 172
Ledford, 177
Lee, 13, 33, 38, 65, 66, 67, 69, 103, 110, 128, 136, 137, 214
Leftwich, 294
Lester, 2, 55, 215
Letcher, 187, 188, 189, 190, 191, 192, 194, 197, 199, 200, 201, 202, 203, 204, 205
Letcher, William, 190, 191, 194, 198, 204
Levering, 15, 316, 317
Librescu, 39, 40, 354
Logathan, 36
Lookabill, 272, 273, 276, 278, 286
Lovall, 255
Lynch Hollow, 9, 150, 151, 152

M

Mann, 308, 310
Marion, 195
Marr, 192
Marshall, 56, 67, 116, 117, 126
Martin, 51, 67, 97, 100, 106, 107, 109, 115, 116, 119, 124, 129, 177, 243, 319, 357
Martinsville, 2, 9, 13, 47, 48, 58, 80, 97, 98, 99, 101, 104, 105, 108, 109, 110, 111, 112, 116, 118, 119, 121, 122, 123, 124, 128, 129, 130, 140, 142, 143, 212, 213, 215, 386
Martinsville Bulletin, 13, 112
Martinsville Seven, 9, 99, 108, 118, 121, 122, 124, 128, 129, 130, 140, 142, 386
Massengill, 357, 360, 361
Massie, 299, 300, 301, 302, 303, 304, 307, 308, 312, 314, 332
Mayberry, 2, 74, 182
Mays, 216, 220
McBryde, 352, 375
McCargo, 175, 178
McCraw, 256, 257, 258, 259, 260, 261, 267, 293, 319
McDonald, 294
Meeks, 200, 202
Merrey, 40
Midkiff, 74, 79
Miller, 25
Millner, 100, 101, 102, 103, 105, 106, 107, 109, 113, 114, 115, 121, 124, 128, 133
Montgomery County, 195, 201
Moody, 176, 178
Moore, 299
Moravians, 82

Morgan, 203
Morva, 33, 360
Mount Airy, 2, 9, 15, 72, 73, 74,
75, 78, 79, 81, 82, 83, 91,
175, 176, 177, 178, 179, 180,
181, 182, 183, 184, 193, 201,
237, 240, 244, 245, 249, 251,
252, 253, 254, 256, 258, 259,
262, 263, 265, 268, 269, 270,
291, 294, 314, 315, 319, 382,
385, 395
Mount Airy Knitting, 9, 252,
253, 256, 262, 263, 265, 269
Mount Airy Times, 176, 385
Mount Airy, North Carolina, 2
Mountjoy, 204
Mulberry Road, 56

N

NAACP, 97, 112, 116, 117,
125, 127
New River, 24, 78, 200, 275,
280, 285, 286
New York Times, 54, 63, 312
New York Yankees, 355, 356
Newman Library, 351, 364,
396, 397
Nichols, 199, 200, 202, 216,
218
Nickelston, 11, 105
Norris, 28, 34, 35, 36, 39, 41,
42, 43, 353, 359, 361, 363,
366, 367, 369, 370
North Carolina Granite
Corporation, 193

O

O'Dell, 37, 366

P

Pannill, 98
Patrick County, 2, 15, 63, 64,
65, 66, 67, 68, 69, 70, 147,
189, 190, 192, 199, 204, 213,
216, 234, 240, 241, 244, 245,
246, 247, 289, 317, 352, 382,
395, 396, 397
Patterson, 261
Paxton, 188
Pedigo, 49, 149
Pence, 366
Penn, 192
Perkins, 189, 190, 192
Perry, 2, 3, 4, 175, 395, 396,
397, 398
Pershing, 36
Petersburg, 187
Petersen, 363
Peterson, 253
Pettie, 100
Phillips, 253, 254, 255, 256,
257, 259, 260, 261, 265
Philpott, 210, 231
Pittsylvania County, 68, 69,
108, 147, 189
Pohle, 37
Prater, 221
Preston, 195, 201
Prillaman, 101
Pryde, 363
Pulaski County, 273, 277, 287

Q

Queen Anne, 292
Quesenberry, 295, 305
Quinn,, 221

R

Radford, 29, 32, 34, 274, 275, 276, 277, 279, 280, 282, 284, 285, 351

Randolph, 194

Raw-Headed-Bloody-Bones, 150

Redd, 100, 101, 107, 114, 115, 130

Republicans, 289, 296

Rex Theater, 100

Reynolds, 62, 65, 66, 67, 69, 70

Richmond, Virginia, 204

Riddle, 200, 202

Ridge, 151, 152, 188, 190, 193, 197, 236, 245, 248, 312, 315, 358

Rives, 55, 67, 68, 69

Roanoke, 26, 30, 51, 68, 108, 209, 312, 313, 337, 366, 367, 385

Robertson, 396, 397

Rock Springs, 65

Roy, 23

S

Saga Magazine, 55

Sale, 121

Samuels, 297, 298, 299, 301, 309

Scotland, 191

Scott, 178, 180, 214

Seaton, 149

Sentman, 78, 79, 80

Shaalan, 36

Shaw, 249

Shelton, 63, 66, 69, 201, 202, 216, 217, 218, 219, 220, 221, 230

Short, 8, 197

Smith, 145, 155, 168, 181, 182, 193, 212, 214, 215, 219, 220, 222, 256

Sood, 358

South Carolina., 195, 202

Southwest Virginia, 396

Spencer, 48, 252, 262, 263

St. Albans, 24, 25, 27, 279, 287

Staples, 64, 68

Steger, 31, 32, 33, 39, 348, 349, 351, 356, 358

Steinbrenner, 356

Sterne, 367

Stewart, 191

Stockton, 236, 237, 238, 239, 240, 241, 242, 243, 244, 245, 246, 247, 248, 249, 251, 385

Stoneman, 398

Stover, 101

Strickland, 358

Stuart, 2, 9, 65, 67, 71, 104, 108, 109, 148, 149, 177, 191, 205, 206, 215, 216, 245, 246, 289, 308, 352, 395, 396, 397

Stuart, Alexander, 203

Stuart, J. E. B., 187, 190, 191, 199, 205

Sumner, 177, 181

Supreme Court, 62, 67, 68, 69, 110, 117, 122, 123, 124, 126, 127, 130, 363

Surry County, North Carolina, 191, 197, 198

T

Tarleton, 51, 195, 203

Tate, 241, 242

Taylor, 65, 103, 104, 106, 107, 109, 113, 121, 129, 138, 149, 165

Terry, 47, 48, 192, 364, 366

Texas, 83, 95, 188, 189, 301, 350

The Baltimore Evening Sun, 312

The Bluefield Daily Telegraph, 312

The Daily Worker, 108

The Danville Register, 123

The Dead Files, 280

The Hollow, 9, 147, 148, 151, 190, 200

The Mount Airy News, 245

Thomas, 2, 3, 73, 75, 76, 77, 78, 84, 85, 86, 87, 89, 90, 190, 193, 195, 293, 294, 297, 298, 310, 355, 396, 397

Thornhill, 29, 30, 32, 34

Till, 117

Tipton, 295, 301

Tolbert, 177

Tories, 187, 194, 196, 197, 198, 199, 200, 201, 202

Tory, 195, 197, 199, 200, 201, 204

Trower, 81

True Detective, 83

Trump, 316, 366

Tuck, 121, 144

Tucker, 116

Turner, 80, 81, 211, 216, 220, 227, 229

U

Underwood, 105

USS Monitor, 210

V

Valencic, 273

Vaughan, 214

Vest, 64

Virginia Ore and Lumber, 222

Virginia Tech, 6, 9, 18, 19, 21, 22, 23, 25, 27, 28, 29, 30, 31, 33, 34, 35, 36, 37, 38, 39, 40, 41, 44, 65, 274, 277, 281, 319, 320, 345, 347, 348, 350, 351, 355, 356, 359, 360, 362, 363, 364, 365, 366, 367, 368, 369, 371, 377, 385, 396, 397

W

Wade, 98, 101, 103, 105, 115, 164, 167

Walker, 165

Walls, 147, 148, 149

Walnut Cove, 160, 166

Walther, 26, 42

Warna, 176

Washington, 201

Washington Nationals, 355

Washington, George, 203

Webb, 78, 79, 80, 81, 292, 296, 300, 302, 303, 304, 305, 306, 307, 308, 314

Wesley Edwards, 294, 311, 314

West Amber Johnston, 28, 38

White, 37, 95, 96, 126, 128, 155, 175, 178, 209, 237, 382

Whitehead, 109

Whittle, 109, 110, 111, 112, 113, 121, 123, 126, 130, 141

Wickham, 218

Widener, 318

Wilburn, 280

Wilder, 247

Williams, 74, 247
Williamson, 209
Wilson, 190
Winston-Salem, 70, 74, 160, 161, 178, 311, 385
Womble, 81
Woodruff, 121
Woolwine, 148

Wooten, 67
Wythe County, 200

Y

Yadkin, 191, 203
Yorktown, 203

Historian Tom Perry at the site he saved, J. E. B. Stuart's Birthplace, the Laurel Hill Farm, just outside Mount Airy in Patrick County, Virginia.

About The Author

J. E. B. Stuart's biographer, Emory Thomas, describes Tom Perry as "a fine and generous gentleman who grew up near Laurel Hill, where Stuart grew up, has founded J. E. B. Stuart Birthplace, and attracted considerable interest in the preservation of Laurel Hill. He has started a symposium series about aspects of Stuart's life to sustain interest in Stuart beyond Ararat, Virginia." Perry graduated from Patrick County High School in 1979 and Virginia Tech in 1983 with a bachelor's degree in history.

Tom founded the J. E. B. Stuart Birthplace in 1990. The non-profit organization has preserved 75 acres of the Stuart property including the house site where J. E. B. Stuart was born on February 6, 1833. Perry wrote the eight interpretive signs about Laurel Hill's history along with the Virginia Civil War Trails sign and the new Virginia Historical Highway Marker in 2002. He spent many years researching and traveling all over the nation to find Stuart materials. He continues his work to preserve Stuart's Birthplace, producing the Laurel Hill Teacher's Guide for educators and the Laurel Hill Reference Guide for groups.

Perry can be seen on Virginia Public Television's Forgotten Battlefields: The Civil War in Southwest Virginia, with his mentor, noted Civil War Historian Dr. James I. Robertson, Jr. Perry has begun a collection of papers relating to Stuart and Patrick County history in the Special Collections Department of the Carol M.

Newman Library at Virginia Tech under the auspices of the Virginia Center for Civil War Studies.

Historian Thomas D. Perry is the author and publisher of over forty books on regional history in Virginia surrounding his home county of Patrick. He is the author of ten books on Patrick County, Virginia, including Ascent to Glory, The Genealogy of J. E. B. Stuart, The Free State of Patrick: Patrick County Virginia in the Civil War, The Dear Old Hills of Patrick: J. E. B. Stuart and Patrick County, Virginia, Images of America: Patrick County Virginia, and Notes From The Free State Of Patrick.

For a decade, Perry taught Civil War history to every eleventh-grade history class at his alma mater, Patrick County High School, from his book The Free State of Patrick: Patrick County Virginia in the Civil War. He can be seen on Henrico County Virginia's DVD documentary Bold Dragoon: The Life of J. E. B. Stuart.

http://henrico-va.granicus.com/MediaPlayer.php?clip_id=1088

Perry was a featured presenter at the Virginia Festival of the Book in 2012. He speaks all over the country on topics as far ranging as Andy Griffith to J. E. B. Stuart.

In 2004, Perry began The Free State of Patrick Internet History Group, which became the largest historical organization in the area, with over 500 members. It covered Patrick County, Virginia, and regional history. Tom produced a monthly email newsletter about regional history entitled Notes From The Free

State of Patrick that comes from his website,

In 2009, Perry used his book Images of America Henry County Virginia to raise over $25,000 for the Bassett Historical Center, "The Best Little Library in Virginia," and as editor of the Henry County Heritage Book raised another $30,000. Perry was responsible for over $200,000 of the $800,000 raised to expand the regional history library.

He is the recipient of the John E. Divine Award from the Civil War Education Association, the Hester Jackson Award from the Surry County Civil War Round Table, and the Best Article Award from the Society of North Carolina Historians for his article on Stoneman's Raid in 2008. In 2010, he received acknowledgment from the Bassett Public Library Association for his work to expand the Bassett Historical Center and was named Henry County Virginia Man of the Year by www.myhenrycounty.com. The Sons of the American Revolution presented Tom with the Good Citizenship Award. Perry also recently received the National Society of the Daughters of the American Revolution Community Service Award from the Patrick Henry Daughters of the American Revolution.

Perry has remembered the history of those who helped him. He worked with the Virginia Department of Transportation to name the bridge over the Dan River after his neighbor, Command Sergeant Major Zeb Stuart Scales, who was the most decorated non-commissioned soldier from Patrick County, Virginia. Perry

remembered his teachers at Blue Ridge Elementary School

including his father, Erie Perry, who was a teacher and principal

for thirty years in The Free State of Patrick, by placing a

monument to the retired teachers at the school in Ararat, Virginia.

Perry, a recognized authority on J. E. B. Stuart is presently

working on a three volume projected titled The Papers of J. E. B.

Stuart.

The Sidna Allen House seen as murder in a rear view mirror.

Made in the USA
Lexington, KY
23 November 2019